W9-AWG-935

Offshoring in the Global Economy

Offshoring in the Global Economy

Microeconomic Structure and Macroeconomic Implications

Robert C. Feenstra

The MIT Press
Cambridge, Massachusetts
London, England

© 2010 Massachusetts Institute of Technology

All rights reserved. No part of this book may be reproduced in any form by any electronic or mechanical means (including photocopying, recording, or information storage and retrieval) without permission in writing from the publisher.

MIT Press books may be purchased at special quantity discounts for business or sales promotional use. For information, please email special_sales @mitpress.mit.edu or write to Special Sales Department, The MIT Press, 55 Hayward Street, Cambridge, MA 02142.

This book was set in Palatino by Toppan Best-set Premedia Limited and was printed and bound in the United States of America.

Library of Congress Cataloging-in-Publication Data

Feenstra, Robert C.
Offshoring in the global economy: microeconomic structure and macroeconomic implications / Robert C. Feenstra.
     p. cm.—(Ohlin lectures)
Includes bibliographical references and index.
ISBN 978-0-262-01383-3 (hardcover : alk. paper)
1. Contracting out. 2. Offshore outsourcing. 3. Wages–Effect of international trade on. I. Title.
HD2365.F44   2010
338.6'3–dc22

                                                        2009027343

10 9 8 7 6 5 4 3 2

Contents

Preface

Starting in the early 1990s, it was noticed that the wages of low-skilled workers relative to high-skilled workers in the United States had fallen in the previous decade. This observation captured the attention of trade and labor economists alike, leading to a sometimes heated exchange on the role of trade versus technological change in explaining wage movements. That discussion continues today but has changed in form, now focusing on workers in the middle of the wage distribution who appear to have lost ground relative to others.

In lecture 1, I begin with the contrasting views of two trade economists—Paul Krugman and Edward Leamer—since the lessons from their exchange help us understand the most recent literature today. Despite their differences both relied on an underlying Heckscher–Ohlin structure in which countries trade final goods. I will suggest that neither of them could adequately explain the wages movements of the 1980s, and because of that, their debate spawned a new type of trade model focusing on the transfer of production processes across countries: these are models of foreign outsourcing or offshoring. The extent to which these models are really new, or simply a re-casting of Heckscher–Ohlin intuition, serves to frame the discussion.

I review my early work with Gordon Hanson (Feenstra and Hanson 1996, 1997, 1999), and also the more recent model by Gene Grossman and Esteban Rossi-Hansberg (2008a, b). At first glance these models appear to give different results, but on closer inspection this contrast can be traced to differing assumptions, much as in the debate between Krugman and Leamer. Moreover I argue that the remaining differences between the models neatly capture the alternative experience of US manufacturing during the 1980s and 1990s, as materials offshoring has given way to services offshoring. Thus this lecture both "closes the gap" between these models and points out where they best apply in practice. I conclude the lecture by suggesting a new calculation of the factor content of trade, which enables us to overcome the aggregation bias noted by Krugman (2008) and serves to show how this Heckscher–Ohlin calculation can still be used to measure the importance of offshoring.

In lecture 2, I deal with less familiar territory—the macroeconomic implications of offshoring. My discussion there focuses on three potential implications: business cycle volatility, prices, and productivity. The material on business cycle volatility draws on my work with Paul Bergin and Gordon Hanson (Bergin, Feenstra, and Hanson 2007, 2009a, b), while the work on prices and exchange rates draws on Bergin and Feenstra (2009). Both of these topics illustrate the usefulness of microeconomic trade models to analyze macroeconomic phenomena, as has also been recognized by many other scholars in the field. It is natural to expect that the flexible production patterns inherent in the outsourcing or offshoring of tasks can lead to fluctuations across borders and, in that way, amplify volatility. If we add to this model the realistic idea that firms charge variable markups, then we also obtain a reason for trade to influence prices and exchange rate pass-through. The third topic covered in this chapter—productivity—pertains to the measurement of productivity growth by statistical agencies. Based on joint work with Marshall Reinsdorf and Matthew Slaughter (Feenstra, Reinsdorf, and Slaughter 2008), I argue that the speedup in productivity growth in the United States during the second half of the 1990s is due in part to a terms of trade improvement. Those results are now being updated in joint work with Benjamin Mandel (Feenstra et al. 2009).

Both lectures appear in much the same form that I presented them at the Stockholm School of Economics on September 17 and 18, 2008. I wish to thank Mats Lundahl for the generous invitation to present the Ohlin Lectures, along with two reviewers who provided insightful comments on the lectures. One of those comments was to add more to the conclusions, and in particular, to suggest directions for further research. So in this manuscript I have added such a chapter, drawing on material presented at the lectures along with some new material. That final chapter deals with both empirical and theoretical results, pointing to promising new research as well as to intriguing puzzles that have not yet been addressed. It is my hope that this final chapter, in conjunction with the lectures themselves, can stimulate further inquiry on the global effects of offshoring.

Lecture 1: Microeconomic Structure

Bertil Ohlin, building on the pioneering contributions of Eli Heckscher, wrote shortly after the first golden age of trade, which lasted from about 1890 to the beginning of World War I. In this period dramatic improvements were being made in transportation, particularly in steamship and rail transport, and with the addition of wireless communication, that greatly facilitated increases in international trade. It is no surprise then that Heckscher and Ohlin were led to modify the assumptions of the Ricardian model of trade, and to suppose that technologies would spread quickly between countries while resource endowments would be the domestic constraint. Their ideas ushered in a new era of trade theory that dominated academic work after World War II.

We are arguably now in a second golden age of trade. As in the first golden age, technological improvements in transport and communications have led to declines in costs of container shipping, and developing countries can now leapfrog to fiber optic cable and cellular telephone services at costs lower than in advanced economies. These costs have now fallen so much that it is possible to break apart the production process, with various stages occurring in different countries. This is the idea of "fragmentation," as Ronald

Jones (2000) referred to it in his Ohlin Lecture a decade ago. There are innumerable examples of this fragmentation of the production process, which is alternatively described as "foreign outsourcing," or simply "offshoring," the term that has become popular and that I will use.

The ability to utilize labor in other countries suggests that domestic resources are no longer the binding constraint on international trade. This new feature of globalization means that the spread of technology is even more rapid than in the time of Heckscher and Ohlin. The speed with which instructions and designs can be transmitted overseas further suggests that these activities need not occur in the same country as production, but that firms can truly search the global economy in order to minimize costs. We might expect therefore that a new paradigm is needed to describe this second golden age of trade.

Or is it? Is the Heckscher–Ohlin (HO) model—in all its manifestations—sufficiently rich to guide our understanding of offshoring, or does it leave out some critical elements? That will be an organizing theme for my lectures. To answer this question we might look first at the microeconomic structure of the models being used. I use the term "microeconomic structure" in the same sense as Ronald Jones in his classic 1965 article ("The Structure of Simple General Equilibrium Models"), to refer to features like the number of goods included in the model, the number of factors, whether we are treating world prices as fixed or not, and so forth. It will turn out that these simple assumptions make a huge difference to the results obtained. To see this, we can look at the writings of trade economists in this area.

I will start with the debate between Edward Leamer (1994) and Paul Krugman (2000) that took place in the mid-1990s, focusing on the issue of whether technology or trade explained the change in wages in the United States. These scholars used differing assumptions on the microeconomic structure, as I will discuss, and therefore reached different conclusions. But it is noteworthy that neither Leamer nor Krugman arrived at a satisfactory explanation for the change in wages that occurred in the 1980s. During this decade there was a pronounced shift in the pattern of wages earned by workers in the United States and other countries: relative wages shifted toward more-skilled workers, so that a "wage gap" developed between those with higher and lower skills. The Stolper–Samuelson theorem would lead us to expect that the movement in world prices could have such an impact on factor prices, but Leamer (1998) rejects that explanation for the 1980s. Alternatively, factor-content calculations might explain the fall in low-skilled wages as due to increased imports in the United States, especially by developing countries, but Krugman (2000, 2008) also finds that this explanation is insufficient. Both these negative findings create puzzles that can and should be addressed by later research.

The debate between Leamer and Krugman can be explained with a very simple version of the HO model, relying on two goods and two factors. My own work with Gordon Hanson (1996, 1997, 1999) adopts instead a Heckscher–Ohlin structure with a continuum of goods. In that case it turns out that the pattern of wage changes in the 1980s is entirely consistent with international trade, and in particular, the changes in prices are consistent with the changes in wages. So Hanson and I address the Stolper–Samuelson puzzle raised by Leamer, at least for the 1980s. But the story for the 1990s is much different. There has continued to be an increase in the relative wage of skilled workers in US manufacturing, but the relative employment of these workers has fallen. That finding is strongly suggestive of the offshoring of service activities whereby the more routine service activities are sent overseas. While this is a new phenomenon in the United States, it has applied to Sweden and other European countries for quite some time.

To explain this new form of offshoring, I will appeal to the recent work of Gene Grossman and Esteban Rossi-Hansberg (2008a, b), emphasizing what they call "trade in tasks." They present their model of offshoring as a new paradigm, so we should examine how it differs from my earlier work with Hanson and therefore from a many-good Heckscher–Ohlin model. I will argue that in the case of offshoring the tasks performed by low-skilled labor, the results obtained by Grossman and Rossi-Hansberg (2008a) are broadly similar to those in my earlier work with Hanson; and furthermore the differences between us and them echo some of the same issues of microeconomic structure that arose in the debate between Leamer and Krugman. However, when we consider instead the offshoring of tasks that use *high-skilled labor*, like service tasks, then their framework can provide results that are different from my earlier work but consistent with the recent empirical observations for the United States.

I will conclude this lecture by returning to the puzzle raised by Krugman: why the factor-content calculations are not able to explain the pattern of wage changes in the United States. In his very recent paper for the Brooking Institution, Krugman (2008) speculates that the failure of the factor-content approach may be due to aggregation bias: computing factor contents at an aggregate level that hides their true magnitudes. I will confirm this idea, and present some new calculations of the factor-content of trade for the United States. These calculations confirm the relevance of the Heckscher–Ohlin model even in the presence of offshoring, and the continued relevance of that model to trade in the global economy today.

Outsourcing versus Offshoring

The terms "foreign outsourcing" and "offshoring" are often used interchangeably, so it is useful at the outset to define these terms carefully. Consider a firm that it making a decision about where and how to engage a portion of its production process: the assembly of components, for example, or research and development. The choices of this firm can be represented as in figure 1.1. Along the top of the diagram are the two possible locations where the firm can decide to engage this production, namely at home or in a foreign country. Along the side of the diagram are the ways that the firm can decide whether to keep the process within the firm or contract with another firm. In the case where the process is kept at home (i.e., in-house), we have "integration" within the firm; whereas if the process is kept at home but outsourced, we have "domestic outsourcing." If instead the

Location of production process

		Home country	Foreign country
Ownership of production process	In-house	Integration	Multinational
	Outsource	Domestic outsourcing	Foreign outsourcing

Figure 1.1
Organization choices for the firm

production process is sent abroad but kept in-house, then production corresponds to what occurs within a "multinational firm," and in the final case where production is sent abroad but outside the firm, we have the case of "foreign outsourcing." So the diagram of figure 1.1 exhausts four possibilities of production.

Where does "offshoring" enter the picture? A narrow definition of offshoring, used sometimes in business circles, describes what occurs when a firm sends a portion of its production process abroad but keeps it in-house. The firm then becomes a multinational: this is the upper-right-hand cell in figure 1.1. By this narrow definition, offshoring is distinct from foreign outsourcing as a strategy of the firm. But a more common definition of "offshoring" is that it encompasses both the multinational strategy *and* foreign outsourcing, meaning it refers to any transfer of production overseas, whether it is done within or outside the firm.[1] By this definition, "offshoring" encompasses both choices in the right-hand column of figure 1.1, and following Grossman and Rossi-Hansberg (2008a, b), I will use this broad definition of offshoring.

There has been a great deal of research in international trade on the organizational choices of the firm illustrated in figure 1.1. The decision of whether to locate activities inside or outside the firm is analyzed using a theory of the boundaries of the firm. One popular theory is the property-rights approach of Grossman, Hart, and Moore (Grossman and Hart 1986; Hart and Moore 1990). By this theory, firms are just collections of agents; some of these agents are engaged in production (call them workers) and others sell the final good (call them managers). Both parties obtain disutility from exerting effort, and it is assumed that it is impossible to write a contract for payment contingent on these efforts.

Because the first-best, competitive outcome cannot be obtained, under Nash bargaining workers and managers share the surplus (or profits). As a result there is an inherent inefficiency in the amount of effort each party is willing to exert.

One way to offset this inefficiency is to break apart the firm so that the production processes are outsourced. Workers engaged in outsourced production are self-employed, so they have more incentive to exert high effort. Still the first-best is not achieved in cases where the self-employed workers are subject to a "holdup" problem: the firm they are selling to cannot credibly promise to pay them at first-best level for their output (because no contracts exist), so their production efforts are only second best. Conversely, the firm that integrates production raises the incentives of managers (who are technically owners) because, with property rights, managers have the residual right of control over all assets. In particular, this means that managers have the right to seize the output of workers performing the tasks that are, in this case, integrated. Because of the outside option to outsource for owners should Nash bargaining break down, this raises their efforts as well but diminishes the incentive for workers employed in the integrated firm.

Clearly, in terms of effort levels, outsourcing and integration affect differently the incentives of the two parties. Depending on which organizational choice gives the highest joint surplus, the firm will or will not choose to integrate production. This framework of worker/manager incentives has a natural application in international trade where we can assume that the difficulties in enforcing contracts are greater *across* countries than *within* a country. For example, Antràs (2003) finds that contracting problems and Nash bargaining only occur *across* countries and, furthermore, only affect the labor-intensive portion of production. The capital-intensive portion is performed in the North, but wages are cheaper in the South, so the firm choosing to shift the labor-intensive portion of production there faces the inefficiencies I have discussed. Antràs (2003) argues that it is optimal for highly capital-intensive Northern firms to keep Southern production in-house, namely to operate as a multinational and leave more labor-intensive Northern firms to outsource production activity South. Antràs (2005) extends this model to allow for exogenous reductions in the capital-share parameter as the product matures, leading to a natural product cycle as the firm moves from the North to the South, and from integration to outsourcing. Antràs and Helpman (2004) add heterogeneity in the productivity of Northern firms, allowing for a more complete choice structure among the four organizational forms displayed in figure 1.1. These papers and many others dealing with the organization of the global firm are summarized in Helpman (2006) and Helpman, Marin, and Verdier (2008).

In these lectures, I do not deal with the outsourcing decision, but only the choice of whether or not to offshore. The first model I will discuss, which is due to Feenstra and Hanson (1996, 1997), has arm's-length transactions between firms at home and abroad. Both factor prices and technologies differ across countries. In Feenstra and Hanson, we refer to this as a "foreign outsourcing" model, which is accurate in the sense that the parties involved are at arm's length: the choice is whether to shift more activities overseas--this means moving between the left and right cells at the bottom row of figure 1.1. Following that model, I will discuss the more recent model of Grossman and Rossi-Hansberg (2008a), which also has factor prices differing across countries. Foreign technology differs from that at home, but if the domestic firm shifts production abroad, then it *carries with it the home technology*. For that reason we might think of this model as applying to a home firm shifting its own technology abroad, without suffering any adverse consequences from sharing the technology with a foreign partner. In other words, the model can be interpreted as the choice between the left and right cells on the top row of figure 1.1, as whether a domestic integrated firm should become a multinational instead. I stress that this is only an interpretation, as the ownership structure in Grossman and Rossi-Hansberg (2008a), and in Feenstra and Hanson (1996, 1997), is not explicitly discussed. Despite these differing interpretations of the models, we should think of both of them as just analyzing the offshoring decision, which is my focus in these lectures.

Evidence from US Manufacturing

Let us start with the pattern of wages over time in the United States. In figures 1.2 and 1.3, I use data from the manufacturing sector to measure the wages of "nonproduction" workers relative to "production" workers. As these terms suggest, nonproduction workers are involved in service activities while production workers are involved in the manufacture and assembly of goods. These two categories can also be called "nonmanual" and "manual" or "white collar" and "blue collar." Generally, nonproduction workers require more education, so we will regard these workers as skilled and production workers as less skilled.

In figure 1.2, notice that the earnings of nonproduction relative to production workers moved erratically from the late 1950s to the late 1960s, and from that point until the early 1980s, relative wages were on a downward trend. It is

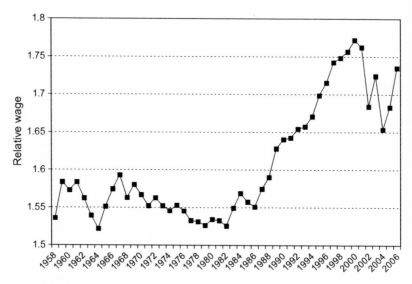

Figure 1.2
Relative wage of nonproduction/production workers, US manufacturing,
1958 to 2006. Source: National Bureau of Economic Research productivity
database, updated after 1996 from Bureau of the Census.

generally accepted that the relative wage fell during this
period because of an increase in the supply of college gradu-
ates, namely skilled workers who moved into nonproduction
jobs. Starting in the early 1980s, however, this trend reversed
itself and the relative wage of nonproduction workers
increased steadily to 2000, with erratic movements there-
after. The same increase in the relative wages of skilled
workers has been found for other industrial and developing
countries.

Turning to figure 1.3, notice that there has been a steady
increase in the ratio of nonproduction to production workers
through the end of the 1980s, but then a fall in the 1990s,

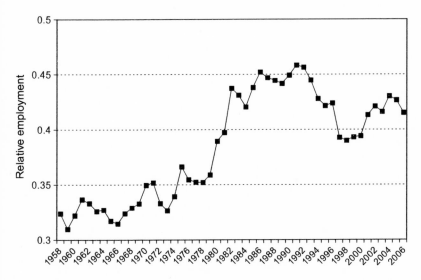

Figure 1.3
Relative employment of nonproduction/production workers, US manufacturing, 1958 to 2006. Source: National Bureau of Economic Research productivity database, updated after 1996 from Bureau of the Census.

which has had some recovery since 2000. The increase in the relative supply of workers throughout the 1970s can account for the *reduction* in the relative wage of nonproduction workers during that decade, as shown in figure 1.2, but this is at odds with the *increase* in the relative nonproduction wage during the 1980s. The rising relative wage should have led to a shift in employment *away* from skilled workers, along the demand curve, but it did not. The only explanation consistent with these facts is that there was an *outward shift* in the demand for more-skilled workers during the 1980s, leading to an increase in their relative employment and wages, as shown in figure 1.4.

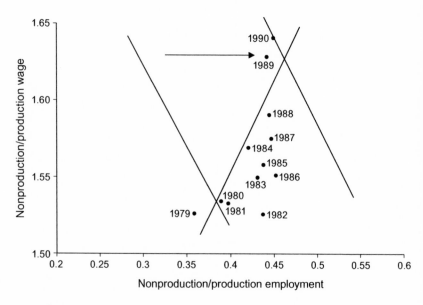

Figure 1.4
Relative wage and employment of nonproduction/production workers in US manufacturing, 1979 to 1990. Source: National Bureau of Economic Research productivity database.

What factors could have led to an outward shift in the relative demand for skilled labor? Such a shift could have come from the increased use of computers and other high-tech equipment or from *skill-biased technological change*. Researchers such as Berman, Bound, and Griliches (1994) argued that technological change was the dominant explanation for the rising relative wage of skilled labor in the United States and other countries. Their reason for rejecting international trade as an explanation was their finding that the majority of increase in manufacturing wage and employment of nonproduction workers was caused by shifts *within* industries and not by shifts *between* industries. That is, the outward shift of relative demand illustrated in figure 1.4 applied to many individual industries, as well as in the aggregate. In their view, the Heckscher-Ohlin model could be ruled out as an explanation because, in that model, the shift would be expected between industries instead of within industries.

Their findings for the United States were reinforced by the work of Berman, Bound, and Machin (1998) who looked at cross-country data. They saw that the same shift toward skilled workers in the United States occurred abroad. That again appeared to rule out the Heckscher–Ohlin model as an explanation, since in that model, when comparing autarky to free trade, we expect wages to move in opposite directions between countries as factor price equalization occurs. The evidence instead was that wages were moving in the same direction across countries—with an increase in the relative wage of skilled workers.

And it was not just labor economists who felt that skill-biased technological change was the dominant reason for the shift in labor demand toward more-skilled workers. That explanation is favored, for example, by the eminent economist Jagdish Bhagwati. Writing in the *Financial Times*, he states:[2]

The culprit is not globalization but labour-saving technical change that puts pressure on the wages of the unskilled. Technical change prompts continual economies in the use of unskilled labour. Much empirical argumentation and evidence exists on this.

For empirical evidence Bhagwati cites Paul Krugman's and my work, as well as the work of labor economists George Borjas and Larry Katz. I will, however, argue that my views have always favored a trade-based explanation and that those of Krugman and others may be changing.

But before making these arguments it is best to go back to the beginning of the debate on trade and wages, to examine the initial response of trade economists to the idea that skill-biased technological change was the dominant explanation.

Factor Bias versus Sector Bias of Technological Change

Edward Leamer (1994, 1998) was among the first trade economists to contribute to the trade versus technology debate. He rejected the claim that skill-biased technological change can explain the shifts in wages for the United States because, in his view, the factor bias of technical change is not important: only the *sector bias* matters. To make this argument, he starts with the zero-profit conditions for industries $i = 1, \ldots, N$, which are written using familiar notation as

$$p_i = \sum_{j=1}^{M} a_{ij} w_j, \qquad i = 1, \ldots, N.$$

Differentiating these and allowing for exogenous changes in the factor requirements a_{ij}, we obtain

$$\hat{p}_i = \sum_{j=1}^{M} \theta_{ij} \hat{w}_j + \sum_{j=1}^{M} \theta_{ij} \hat{a}_{ij}, \qquad i = 1, \ldots, N.$$

The second term above is the negative of total factor productivity growth, which is

$$TFP_i \equiv \hat{y}_i - \sum_{j=1}^{M} \theta_{ij} \hat{x}_{ij} = -\sum_{j=1}^{M} \theta_{ij} \hat{a}_{ij}.$$

Therefore the differentiated zero-profit conditions are stated as follows:

$$\hat{p}_i + TFP_i = \sum_{j=1}^{M} \theta_{ij}\hat{w}_j, \qquad i = 1, \dots, N.$$

Now suppose that the country is small so that prices do not change. Then it is immediate from this equation that the sector bias of technological change, or TFP_i, will determine the change in factor prices. This argument is illustrated simply in figure 1.5, where low-skilled labor earns the wage of w and high-skilled labor earns the wage of q. Suppose that there is technological progress affecting *either* factor in industry 2, which is skilled-labor intensive. Then that industry can afford to pay more to both factors, so its zero-profit contour shifts up, moving the equilibrium from point A to B. Correspondingly the wage earned by skilled labor rises and the wage for unskilled labor falls, regardless of whether the technological progress was biased toward one factor or the other. That is the point that Leamer is making.

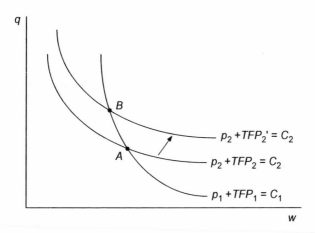

Figure 1.5
Technical progress in sector 2

This relationship between changes in prices and wages is called the "mandated wage equation," and it is estimated as a regression of the log change in industry prices on factor shares:

$$\Delta \ln p_{it} + TFP_{it} = \sum_{j=1}^{M} \frac{1}{2}(\theta_{ijt} + \theta_{ijt-1})\beta_j, \qquad i = 1, \ldots, N.$$

The regression coefficients β are the "mandated" changes in factor prices that are consistent with a competitive economy, and therefore consistent with the Stolper–Samuelson theorem. We can say that the Stolper–Samuelson theorem is validated by the data provided that the estimates β of the factor-price changes are close to their true values for the economy.

When estimating this regression for the United States, Leamer and other authors[3] often find estimates of β that are quite far off the mark: they do not reflect the actual change in wages that occurred and are rather sensitive to the data used and specification of the regression.[4] I believe there is a good explanation for why this regression does not work as well as expected, as will be described in a moment, but first I would like to turn to the response that Krugman gives to Leamer's arguments.

Published in the *Journal of International Economics* in 2000, but written five years earlier, Krugman argues that Leamer's conclusions hold only in a small-country model with fixed world prices, a fact that Leamer is careful to state in qualifying his results.[5] But Krugman goes on to make an important theoretical point: if world prices are endogenously determined, and under the simplifying assumption of Cobb–Douglas preferences, then the sector bias of technological changes completely cancels out and has no impact at all on factor prices. Then only the factor bias matters, contrary to Leamer's arguments.

To make this point, Krugman considers a closed economy with two sectors and two factors—skilled and unskilled labor, where we can assume for convenience that preferences are Cobb–Douglas. Now suppose that either sector has Hicks-neutral technological progress. Then how does that affect the relative demand for labor? The answer is not at all: Hicks-neutral progress lowers the price of that good and raises its demand by just the amount needed to leave factor demands unchanged, as Krugman demonstrates. Since factor demands are unchanged, the relative wage is also unchanged by neutral technological progress. This result continues to hold in a two-country HO model with factor price equalization, provided that the Hicks-neutral technological shift is worldwide.

So in strong contrast to Leamer's small-country case, in the world economy the sector bias of Hicks-neutral technological change does not matter at all. But the factor bias clearly does matter: if either sector has skilled-biased technological change, for example, then the demand for skilled labor shifts out, raising its relative wage. So the large-country case puts the focus squarely back onto the skill bias of technological change.

In the same article Krugman argues that factor content calculations from the HO model are relevant, and that they should be viewed as changes in effective factor endowments in terms of their impact on wages. But it turns out that when this argument is quantified, the actual change in factor contents is just too small to affect wages by anything like the amount observed. So that leaves Krugman with a conundrum, one that I will return to at the end of this lecture.

The conclusions of Leamer (1994) and Krugman (2000) are re-examined and generalized by Xu (2001). Krugman initially derived his results using Leontief technologies but later argued that this is not important. To see the significance of technology, we follow Xu in writing the cost function in each sector as $c_i(a_i w, b_i q)$, $i = 1, 2$, where w is the wage of unskilled labor, q is the wage of skilled labor, and a_i, b_i are technology parameters affecting each factor. If the technologies were Cobb–Douglas, then the cost function becomes

$$c_i(a_i w, b_i q) = (a_i w)^{\alpha_i} (b_i q)^{1-\alpha_i} = A_i w^{\alpha_i} q^{1-\alpha_i}, \text{ with } A_i \equiv (a_i^{\alpha_i} b_i^{1-\alpha_i}).$$

Thus any change in the parameters a_i and b_i is *equivalent* to a Hicks-neutral technological change in the parameters A_i. So, to even discuss the factor bias of technological change, we need to rule out Cobb–Douglas technologies.

As in Hicks (1932) we can define a technological change to be *skill biased* if it raises the relative demand for skilled labor (at constant factor prices). Xu (2001) shows that if the elasticity of substitution between factor σ_i is less than unity, then a *fall in a_i* corresponds to skill-biased technological progress; whereas if σ_i exceeds unity then a *fall in b_i* corresponds to skill-biased technological progress. We will generally focus on the first case, where the elasticity of substitution is less than unity. In the model we review next, from Feenstra and Hanson (1996, 1997), the elasticity of substitution is zero; later when we examine Grossman and Rossi-Hansberg (2008a), we will see that $\sigma_i < 1$ is needed to obtain certain results. Xu (2001) further shows how Krugman's conclusions are sensitive to the assumption that the factor bias of technological change is *worldwide*, and this feature will also turn out to be important in my discussion of Grossman and Rossi-Hansberg (2008a).

Offshoring versus Technological Change

Summing up, neither Leamer nor Krugman arrived at a satisfactory explanation for the change in wages that occurred in the 1980s. But even if a simple two-good, two-factor model cannot explain the shift in relative labor demand toward skilled labor, perhaps a more general specification of the Heckscher–Ohlin model can. Feenstra and Hanson (1996, 1997) present a model of an industry in which there are many "activities," denoted by z, arranged along a "value chain." For convenience we arrange these activities in increasing order of their ratio of skilled to unskilled labor used in each activity. The structure of this model is very similar to a Heckscher–Ohlin model with a continuum of goods, as in Dornbusch, Fischer, and Samuelson (1980), except that we now think of all these activities as taking place within the same industry.

Formally we specify the unit costs of each activity as

$$c(w, q, r, z) = B[wa_L(z) + qa_H(z)]^\theta r^{1-\theta},$$

with the same technologies used in the foreign country, except that we allow the countrywide technology parameter B^* to differ from B. Notice that the portion of the cost function dealing with labor is linear in the wages of unskilled and skilled labor, w and r, and this corresponds to a Leontief technology between these factors, with the fixed requirements $a_L(z)$ and $a_H(z)$ for each unit of output. The outputs $x(z)$ from these activities are combined in a Cobb–Douglas fashion to produce a single, final good:

$$Y = \int_0^1 \alpha(z)x(z)dz.$$

Suppose that relative wage of skilled labor is higher in
the foreign country and that the rental on capital is also
higher:

$$\frac{q}{w} < \frac{q^*}{w^*} \quad \text{and} \quad r < r^*.$$

Then just as in the Heckscher–Ohlin model with a continuum
of goods, in a trade equilibrium we find that countries spe-
cialize in different portions of the skill continuum. Under our
assumption that the relative wage of skilled labor is higher
abroad, and that goods are arranged in increasing order of
their skill intensity, the ratio of the home to foreign unit costs
is downward sloping, as shown by the schedule c/c^* in figure
1.6. Foreign production—or offshoring—occurs where the
relative costs at home are greater than unity, in the range
$[0, z')$, whereas home production occurs where the relative

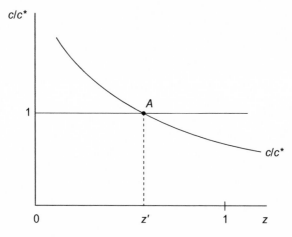

Figure 1.6
Value chain of production

costs at home are less than unity, in the range $(z', 1]$. The borderline activity z' is determined by equal unit costs in the two countries:

$$\frac{c(w, q, r, z')}{c(w^*, q^*, r^*, z')} = 1.$$

Using this unique borderline activity z', we can then calculate the demand for labor in each country. At home, for example, the relative demand for skilled/unskilled labor is

$$D(z') = \frac{\int_{z'}^{1} (\partial c/\partial q) x(z) dz}{\int_{z'}^{1} (\partial c/\partial w) x(z) dz}.$$

It can be shown that this schedule is a downward-sloping function of the relative wage (q/w). A downward-sloping relative demand curve applies to the foreign country too, except now we integrate over the activities in $[0, z')$. In both countries equilibrium factor prices are determined by the equality of relative demand and supply.

Suppose now that the home firm wishes to offshore more activities. The reason for this could be a capital flow from the home to foreign country, reducing the rental abroad and increasing it at home, or alternatively, technological progress abroad that is neutral across all the activities but exceeding such progress at home. In both cases the relative costs of production at home rise, which is an upward shift in the relative cost schedule, as shown in figure 1.7. As a result the borderline between the activities performed at home and abroad shifts from the point z' to the point z^*, with $z^* > z'$.

What is the impact of this increase in offshoring on the relative demand for skilled labor at home and abroad?

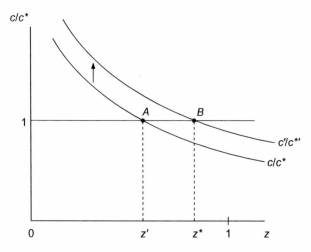

Figure 1.7
Increase in offshoring

Notice that the activities no longer performed at home (those between z' and z^*) are *less* skill intensive than the activities still done there (those to the right of z^*). This means that the range of activities now done at home are more skilled-labor intensive, on average, than the set of activities formerly done at home. For this reason the relative demand for skilled labor at home increases, as occurred in the United States during the 1980s. That increase in demand will also increase the relative wage for skilled labor, as shown in figure 1.8.

What about the impact on in the foreign country? The activities that are newly sent offshore (those between z' and z^*) are *more* skill intensive than the activities that were initially done in the foreign country (those to the left of z'). That means that the range of activities now done abroad is more skilled-labor intensive, on average, than the set of activities

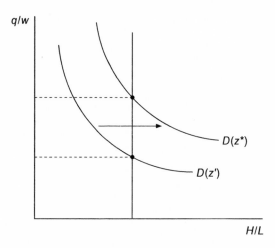

Figure 1.8
Increase in the relative demand for skilled labor

formerly done there. For this reason the relative demand for skilled labor in the foreign country increases, as shown in figure 1.8. With this increase in the relative demand for skilled labor, the relative wage of skilled labor *also* increases in the foreign country. That outcome occurred in as Hong Kong, for example, during the 1980s, as well as in Mexico and other developing countries.

To summarize, this model of Feenstra and Hanson, which borrows the structure of the Heckscher–Ohlin model with a continuum of goods, gives an explanation for the increase in the relative demand for skilled labor that was observed across countries during the 1980s. Of course, this explanation does not *prove* that offshoring was the source of the wage changes, since *skill-biased technological change* is equally well an explanation. So determining which of these explanations accounts for the changes observed during the 1980s is an empirical question.

To address that question, Feenstra and Hanson (1999) start again with the mandated wage equation suggested by Leamer but modify this equation in a fundamental way. They recognize that in any dataset, the wages paid to skilled and unskilled labor differ across industries. They incorporate those interindustry wage differentials into the model by rewriting the zero-profit conditions as

$$p_i = \sum_{j=1}^{M} a_{ij} w_{ij}, \qquad i = 1, \ldots, N,$$

where the wages w_{ij} now differ across industries i and factors j. Differentiating these zero-profit conditions gives

$$\hat{p}_i + TFP_i = \sum_{j=1}^{M} \theta_{ij} \hat{w}_{ij}, \qquad i = 1, \ldots, N.$$

When this regression is run as a mandated wage equation, we are treating the factor price changes as common across industries, thereby ignoring the interindustry wage differentials. That is, letting $\hat{\bar{w}}_j$ denote the *average* value of the change in factor price j across industries, we are actually running the regression

$$\hat{p}_i + TFP_i = \sum_{j=1}^{M} \theta_{ij} \hat{\bar{w}}_j + \varepsilon_j, \qquad i = 1, \ldots, N,$$

where the error term

$$\varepsilon_j \equiv \sum_{j=1}^{M} \theta_{ij} \left(\hat{w}_{ij} - \hat{\bar{w}}_j \right)$$

reflects the difference between the change in the industry and average factor prices.

When Leamer and other authors ran the mandated wage regression, they ignored the presence of the error term ε_j, which led to a potential bias in the estimated coefficients. But we can in fact construct this error term from data on industry wages as compared to the overall average wage, and incorporate it into our estimation. One way to achieve that is to define a dual measure of *effective* TFP, now using discrete changes in time, as

$$ETFP_{it} \equiv \sum_{j=1}^{M} \frac{1}{2}(\theta_{ijt} + \theta_{ijt-1})\Delta \ln \overline{w}_{jt} - \Delta \ln p_{jt}, \qquad i = 1, \ldots, N.$$

This way the economywide change in wages rather than the industry wages is used to define effective TFP. So the mandated wage equation clearly holds as an identity:

$$\Delta \ln p_{jt} + ETFP_{it} \equiv \sum_{j=1}^{M} \frac{1}{2}(\theta_{ijt} + \theta_{ijt-1})\Delta \ln \overline{w}_{jt}, \qquad i = 1, \ldots, N.$$

Running this regression gives estimated coefficients on the average factor shares that exactly match the economy's average changes in factor prices.

To move beyond this identity and estimate the impact of offshoring or skill-biased technological change on factor prices, Feenstra and Hanson recommend a two-step procedure. First, the change in prices plus effective TFP is regressed on various structural variables Z that we think could affect factor prices:

$$\Delta \ln p_i + ETFP_i = \alpha_0 + \alpha_1 \Delta Z_{1i} + \alpha_2 \Delta Z_{2i}, \qquad i = 1, \ldots, N.$$

Next, the estimated coefficients $\hat{\alpha}_1$ and $\hat{\alpha}_2$ are used to construct the dependent variables for the regressions

$$\hat{\alpha}_1 \Delta Z_{1i} = \sum_{j=1}^{M} \frac{1}{2}(\theta_{ijt} + \theta_{ijt-1})\Delta \ln \beta_{1j}$$

and

$$\hat{\alpha}_2 Z_{2i} = \sum_{j=1}^{M} \frac{1}{2}(\theta_{ijt} + \theta_{ijt-1})\Delta \ln \beta_{2j}, \qquad i = 1, \ldots, N.$$

That is, the portion of price and productivity changes explained by each structural variable is regressed on the factor shares to obtain estimates of the change in factor prices explained by that structural variable.[6]

Consider two such variables: offshoring and the use of high-tech equipment such as computers. Offshoring is measured as the intermediate inputs imported by each industry, whether using a broad definition that includes all imported inputs, or a narrow definition that focuses on imported inputs within the same overall industry (e.g., the automobile industry importing auto parts). Likewise high-technology equipment can be measured either as a fraction of the total capital equipment installed in each industry, or as a fraction of new investment in capital that is devoted to computers and other high-tech devices.

In table 1.1 the results from the broad measure of offshoring are reported for the 1980s (similar results are obtained using the narrow measure). For the first measure of high-tech equipment (i.e., fraction of the capital stock) the results in the first row show that roughly 25 percent of the increase in the relative wage of nonproduction workers is explained by offshoring and about 30 percent of that increase by the growing use of high-tech capital. Both offshoring and the increased use of high-tech capital are important to the actual increase in the relative wage of skilled workers. In the second

Table 1.1
Impact on the relative wage of nonproduction labor in US manufacturing, 1979 to 1990

	Percent of total increase explained by each factor	
Measurement of high-tech equipment	Offshoring	High-tech equipment
Share of the capital stock	21–27%	29–32%
Share of capital flow (new investment)	12%	99%

Source: R. C. Feenstra and G. H. Hanson, 1999, The impact of outsourcing and high-technology capital on wages: Estimates for the U.S., 1979–1990, *Quarterly Journal of Economics* 114(3): 907–40.

row is the other measure of high-tech equipment (i.e., the fraction of new investment). The fraction of high-tech equipment in new investment can explain *nearly all* (99 percent) of the increased relative wage for nonproduction workers; this leaves little room for offshoring to play much of a role (it explains only 12 percent of the increase in the relative wage). These results are lopsided enough that we might be skeptical of using new investment to measure high-tech equipment and therefore prefer the results using the capital stocks.[7]

I mention these final results because labor economists, such as Larry Katz and David Autor (1999), often use high-tech equipment as a fraction of new investment, which explains why they find little scope for international trade to be important in their regressions. Those views might be changing, however. Interviewed for an article in the *New York Times*, David Autor said: "The consensus until recently was that trade was not a major cause of the earnings inequality in this country . . . . That consensus is now being revisited."[8]

Summing up, while both offshoring and high-tech equipment can explain the shift in demand toward nonproduction workers in US manufacturing, the relative contributions of the two measures are sensitive to how we measure high-tech equipment. The results I have reported so far on the *relative* wage of nonproduction workers are only part of the story, however. We should also ask about the *real wages* of nonproduction compared to those of production workers. Regardless of how offshoring affects the relative wages, it is entirely possible for *real wages* of all workers to improve (Feenstra and Hanson 1996, p. 101). Such improvement can occur because offshoring leads to a productivity increase, which lowers the price of the final good. It is quite possible for that drop in price to exceed the fall in the wage of either type of worker so that, in theory, all real wages improve.

The actual data for the real hourly earnings of production workers in US manufacturing are shown in figure 1.9, and these data tell a mixed story. From the mid-1980s to the mid-1990s real earnings of production workers fell. Wages rose in the latter part of the 1990s; by 2003 real earnings were close to their 1980 level, and then started another decline.

To see the impact of offshoring on real wages, let us return to the study by Feenstra and Hanson (1999). The two-step procedure allows us to isolate the impact of offshoring and the increased use of high-tech capital on the real wage, directly from the regression coefficients in the second stage. We focus on the most reliable case where high-tech capital is measured as a share of the capital stock. Table 1.2 reports the estimates of the impact of offshoring during the 1980s on real wages of nonproduction and production workers. For nonproduction workers, we find that offshoring caused their

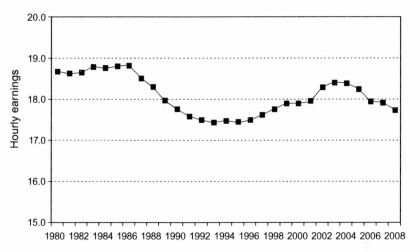

Figure 1.9
Real earnings of production workers, US manufacturing (2008 dollars).
Source: Bureau of Labor Statistics.

Table 1.2
Impact on the real wages of nonproduction and production labor in US manufacturing, 1979 to 1990

	Percentage increase explained by each factor	
Type of labor	Offshoring	High-tech equipment
Real wage of nonproduction workers	1.1–1.8%	2.7–2.8%
Real wage of production workers	0%	0–0.3%

Source: R. C. Feenstra and G. H. Hanson, 1999, The impact of outsourcing and high-technology capital on wages: Estimates for the U.S., 1979–1990, *Quarterly Journal of Economics* 114(3): 907–40.
Note: Annual percentage changes recorded in table V of Feenstra and Hanson (1999) are multiplied by 11 years. High-tech equipment is measured as a share of the capital stock.

real wages to rise between 1 and 2 percent over the entire decade and that increased use of high-technology brought real wages up closer to 3 percent over the same decade. For production workers, we cannot identify any significant impact of offshoring on their real wage, but the increased use of high-tech capital had a very slight positive impact. So for both types of labor, there is no evidence at all that real wages are negatively impacted due to offshoring in the 1980s. These are the results that Jagdish Bhagwati refers to in his writings, to support the view that offshoring does not harm labor.

Offshoring in the 1990s and Services

Let us turn now to the evidence in the United States for the 1990s. The picture for the 1980s is well known from dozens of research studies, but surprisingly, the picture for the 1990s, shown in figure 1.10, is not yet familiar. Notice that from 1989 to 2000, there continued to be an increase in the relative wage of nonproduction/production labor in US manufacturing, but in addition there was a *decrease* in the relative employment of these workers. There are two possible explanations for this shift suggested by the literature. First, some labor economists have argued that the 1990s witnessed a changing pattern of labor demand, benefiting those in the highest and lowest skilled occupations at the expense of others in moderately skilled occupations. Autor, Katz, and Kearney (2008, p. 301) attribute this once again to technological change: "... we find that these patterns may in part be explained by a richer version of the skill-biased technical change (SBTC) hypothesis in which information technology complements highly educated workers engaged in abstract tasks, substitutes for moderately educated workers perform-

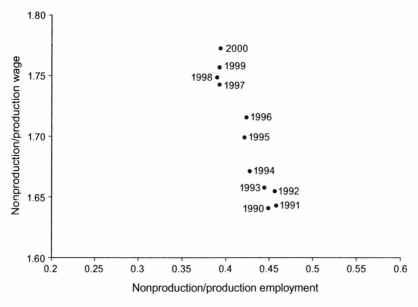

Figure 1.10
Relative wage and employment of nonproduction/production workers in US manufacturing, 1990 to 2000. Source: National Bureau of Economic Research productivity database, updated after 1996 from Bureau of the Census.

ing routine tasks, and has less impact on low-skilled workers performing manual tasks."[9]

A second possibility is that figure 1.10 is a "smoking gun" for service offshoring from US manufacturing. To the extent that the back-office jobs in manufacturing use the lower paid nonproduction workers, the offshoring of those jobs could very well *raise the average* wage among nonproduction workers while lowering their employment. So as we found for the 1980s, once again there are two explanations for the change in wages and employment: the first, emphasized by labor economists drawing on technological change, and the second emphasizing offshoring, but of a different type than was found in the 1980s.

It might be admitted that labor economists arguing that technical change explains the shifting wages, and trade economists suggesting that service offshoring is the reason, are both in danger of relying on an *ad hoc* explanation: with the pattern of wage and employment changes differing from the 1980s, we just change the nature of technological change or offshoring, and still present these as the relevant explanations. To avoid this pitfall, we need to back up the case with compelling theoretical or empirical evidence. Let us first ask whether there is any new theory that can guide us.

It turns out that there is such theory, due to Gene Grossman and Esteban Rossi-Hansberg (2008a). These authors prefer to think of "tasks" performed by high-skilled or low-skilled labor rather than "activities" that combine factors, which is what Feenstra and Hanson (1996, 1997) used. They present a simple two-sector model of the economy where in each sector and for each factor there are a continuum of tasks indexed by $i \in [0,1]$. The production structure is Leontief in the sense that an equal amount of each task must be performed, but the firm can choose whether to do that task at home or offshore it abroad. If the task is offshored, then the home firm uses its *own* technology abroad. While Grossman and Rossi-Hansberg do not specify whether the offshoring is done inside or outside of the firm, the fact that the home technology is transferred abroad suggests a multinational relationship in offshoring.

Consider first low-skilled labor. In each sector j the amount of labor a_{Lj} is needed at home for every task i that is performed, where a_{Lj} depends on the factor prices. If instead the task is offshored, then $\beta t(i) a_{Lj}$ units of low-skilled labor must be employed abroad. The tasks are ordered so that the function $t(i)$ is increasing, as shown in figure 1.11. The amount $[\beta t(i)-1]$ indicates the "extra" labor that must be employed abroad to achieve the same outcome as one unit of labor at home. This formulation is similar to Paul Samuelson's iceberg transport costs, in the sense that it is the services of low-skilled labor that are used up in the offshoring process. We follow Grossman and Rossi-Hansberg in assuming that the offshoring costs $\beta t(i)$ are identical across the two sectors.

The equilibrium amount of offshoring is determined where the costs of performing the borderline task abroad, which is $\beta t(I)w^*$, equals its cost at home,

$$\beta t(I)w^* = w.$$

This equilibrium condition for offshoring needs to be supplemented with the zero-profit and the full-employment conditions. The zero-profit conditions are that the sum of costs of domestic and offshored labor for each unit of production equal the price, or

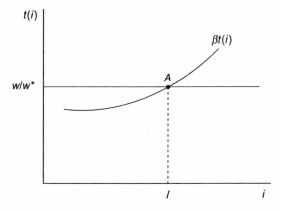

Figure 1.11
Equilibrium with costs of offshoring

$$p_j = wa_{Lj}(1-I) + w^*a_{Lj}\int_0^I \beta t(i)di + qa_{Hj}, \qquad j = 1, 2,$$

where q is the wage of high-skilled labor, which we assume for now is not offshored. Using the equilibrium offshoring condition, zero profits are re-written as

$$p_j = wa_{Lj}\Omega(I) + qa_{Hj}, \qquad j = 1, 2,$$

where

$$\Omega(I) = (1-I) + \int_0^I \frac{t(i)di}{t(I)} < 1.$$

Notice that in this zero-profit condition, offshoring acts just like a low-skilled labor-saving technological innovation, or another form of skill-biased technological change. We can therefore graph two zero-profit conditions to determine the factor prices, as at point A in figure 1.12, recognizing that the iso-cost curves depend on the amount of offshoring.

Suppose now that there is a reduction in the costs of offshoring, which is a fall in β. In figure 1.13 we see an increase in the amount of offshoring as I increases to I' holding wages fixed for the moment. That acts like a low-skilled labor-saving innovation, and it shifts both iso-cost curves to the right horizontally as seen in figure 1.14. A new equilibrium is established where the wage of low-skilled labor has increased while the wage of high-skilled labor is unchanged. The reason for this increase in the low-skilled wage, as emphasized by Grossman and Rossi-Hansberg, is that offshoring acts like a productivity increase for low-skilled labor. That group gains the most from offshoring because their productivity is enhanced: both the real wage and the relative wage of unskilled labor go up.

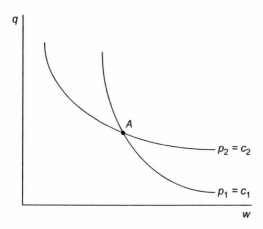

Figure 1.12
Zero-profit equilibrium

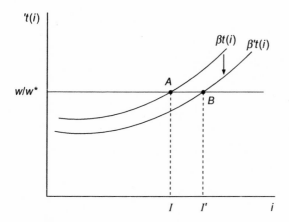

Figure 1.13
Reduction in the costs of offshoring

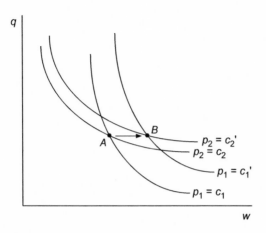

Figure 1.14
Low-skilled labor-saving technical progress

This result received substantial attention when it was presented at the meeting of the Federal Reserve Bank in Jackson Hole, Wyoming, in 2006 (Grossman and Rossi-Hansberg 2006), meriting a write-up in the *Economist* magazine at the time and again in 2007. Let me quote from that article:[10]

> Offshoring makes firms more productive. The tasks that are best kept close to home remain onshore; other tasks can be taken care of in cheaper places abroad. Everyone benefits from this gain in productivity, including workers who have fewer tasks to perform.

I have no problem with the conclusion that the real wages of all workers might rise due to offshoring, so that everyone benefits: that is also a possibility in my model with Hanson. But the prediction that the *relative* wage of low-skilled workers will rise is counterintuitive. That prediction is clearly counterfactual to the experience of the United States and other countries during the 1980s and 1990s. It also contradicts the idea that skill-biased technological change—shifting relative demand toward skilled labor—should increase the relative wage of skilled workers.

To understand where this result is coming from, it is useful to go back to the debate a decade ago between Leamer and Krugman. Leamer (1994, 1998) considered a small-country model in which the sector bias of technical change determines the change in wages. That is exactly what is occurring in this small-country version of the model by Grossman and Rossi-Hansberg. Offshoring acts like low-skilled labor-saving technical progress and has the greatest impact in the sector intensive in low-skilled labor, so the real and relative wages of that factor rises. This idea was also suggested in the fragmentation literature by Sven Arndt (1997) and Jones and Kierzkowski (2001). Their results all confirm Leamer's thesis.

But Krugman would respond that we should instead focus on a large-country model, as Grossman and Rossi-Hansberg do next. In that case we need to take into account how outputs change due to offshoring. The only way the low-skilled labor can remain fully employed at home in the presence of offshoring is for there to be a magnified increase in the output of the low-skilled-intensive sector. That result follows from the Rybczynski theorem, which holds in a modified version here. Since both sectors are offshoring the activities up to I, the full-employment condition for low-skilled labor is

$$y_1 a_{L1}(1-I) + y_2 a_{L2}(1-I) = L,$$

which can be rewritten as

$$y_1 a_{L1} + y_2 a_{L2} = \frac{L}{1-I}.$$

Thus a rise in offshoring will have the same impact on sector outputs as an effective increase in the endowment of low-skilled labor. Through the usual Rybczynski effect this will have a magnified impact on the home output of the low-skilled-intensive good, and thereby also raise that output on world markets and lower its relative price. By the usual Stolper–Samuelson result, that will *reduce* the relative wage of low-skilled labor. So the price effect works against low-skilled labor, whereas the productivity effect of offshoring works in its favor. In general, either of these effects can dominate, so the relative wage can move in either direction.

To sharpen the results, suppose that preferences are Cobb–Douglas, as Krugman (2000) assumed. If production is also Cobb–Douglas, then any technological progress looks like it's Hicks neutral, so we are almost back in Krugman's case where the price effect just offsets the productivity effect, and relative wages do not change at all. That result does not quite hold in Grossman and Rossi-Hansberg's model, even with Cobb–Douglas technologies, because the productivity effect of offshoring applies only in the home country and not abroad. For that reason we need to add more structure to obtain definite results on whether the price effect dominates the productivity effect.

Specifically, we follow Grossman and Rossi-Hansberg in assuming that both industries in the foreign country are uniformly less productive than at home, applying the Hicks-neutral productivity disadvantage $A^* > 1$ abroad. In addition the home country still has the low-skilled labor technological advantage of $\Omega(I) < 1$ due to offshoring, as described above. It is quite possible that there is "adjusted factor price equalization," meaning that $w\Omega = w^*A^*$ and $q = q^*A^*$, as we will assume. The fact that the ratios of effective factor prices $w\Omega/q$ and w^*/q^* are equal across countries means that the factor intensities are also equal, $a_{Lj} = a_{Lj}^*$ and $a_{Hj} = a_{Hj}^*$, $j = 1, 2$, where $A^* a_{Lj}^*$ and $A^* a_{Hj}^*$ are the foreign labor requirements per unit of output. The cost shares are then $\theta_{Lj} \equiv w \Omega a_{Lj} / p_j = w^* A^* a_{Lj}^* / p_j$ for low-skilled labor, and $\theta_{Hj} \equiv q a_{Hj} / p_j = q^* A^* a_{Hj}^* / p_j$ for high-skilled labor, $j = 1, 2$.

With this notation we can state the conditions under which the price effect dominates the productivity effect, so that the relative wage of high-skilled labor rises with offshoring, or when we obtain the converse result (as proved in the appendix):

Proposition 1.1   Suppose that demand in both countries is Cobb–Douglas, with expenditure shares on the two goods of α_j, $j = 1, 2$. If the elasticities of substitution in production σ_j are sufficiently less than unity and the home country is sufficiently large, so that the following inequality holds,

$$\sigma_j < \frac{L/\Omega}{(L/\Omega)+(L^*/A^*)} - \left\{ \frac{L^*/A^*}{(L/\Omega)+(L^*/A^*)} \left[\frac{\alpha_1 \alpha_2 (\theta_{H1} - \theta_{H2})^2}{\alpha_1 \theta_{H1} \theta_{L1} + \alpha_2 \theta_{H2} \theta_{L2}} \right] \right\},$$
$$\text{for } j = 1, 2,$$

then the price effect dominates the productivity effect and the relative wage of high-skilled labor rises with increased offshoring. If this inequality is reversed for $j = 1, 2$, then the relative wage of high-skilled labor falls.

We see that a *necessary* condition to obtain a rise in the relative wage of high-skilled labor is that the elasticities of substitution in production are less than unity (as obtained from the inequality above as $L \to \infty$). This condition follows from our earlier discussion of Xu (2001): since offshoring acts like low-skilled labor-saving technical progress, this will shift relative demand *away* from that factor and toward high-skilled labor if and only if $\sigma_j < 1.$[11] That condition is necessary but not sufficient, however, because only the home country is experiencing the effective technical progress due to off-shoring. Therefore we need the *added condition* that the home country is large enough compared to the foreign country that the inequality in proposition 1.1 is satisfied. Under these conditions we obtain the results of Krugman (2000), that skill-biased technological change will raise the relative wage of high-skilled labor, which is like the results of Feenstra and Hanson (1996, 1997), who assumed that the elasticities of substitution in production are zero. Conversely, if the inequality in proposition 1.1 is reversed, then the productivity effect necessarily dominates the price effect, and the relative wage of high-skilled labor will fall due to offshoring. That is the result obtained in the small-country version of the model.

Even without Cobb–Douglas preferences, results similar to the large-country case (with elasticities of substitution less than unity) occur if there are more factors than goods. For example, suppose there is only a single good in both countries. That good will still be traded to compensate for the labor earnings from offshoring. For this particular case, Grossman and Rossi-Hansberg argue that there is a third effect at work, which they call the labor-supply effect. The effective increase in low-skilled labor due to the productivity effect cannot be absorbed by Rybczynski-like reallocation across sectors, so instead the relative wage of low-skilled labor will fall. If the initial amount of offshoring is small, the labor-supply effect will definitely dominate the productivity effect, and the relative wage of low-skilled labor will fall as a result. Once again, its real wage can move in either direction, while the real wage of high-skilled labor rises.

So we see that the microeconomic structure of the model—small country versus large country, and the number of sectors as compared with factors—is crucial to the results.[12] The large-country version has predictions that fit the facts for the United States in the 1980s. But the 1990s were different, as an increase in the relative wage of nonproduction workers occurred with a *fall* in their relative demand. I have already suggested that the evidence is consistent with the offshoring of service activities from the United States, or the lower paid of the nonproduction tasks. That outcome can also arise in the model of Grossman and Rossi-Hansberg, provided that we focus on the offshoring of *high-skilled* labor tasks rather than *low-skilled* tasks.

With offshoring of high-skilled labor, the equilibrium condition becomes $q^*\beta t(I) = q$. The zero-profit conditions are that the sum of the costs of domestic and offshored labor for each unit of production equal the price, or

$$p_j = wa_{Lj} + qa_{Hj}(1-I) + q^* a_{Hj} \int_0^I \beta t(i)di, \qquad j = 1, 2.$$

Using the equilibrium offshoring condition, zero profits, we can rewrite this as

$$p_j = wa_{Lj} + qa_{Hj}\Omega(I), \qquad j = 1, 2,$$

where $\Omega(I) < 1$ is defined as before.

Now offshoring acts just like a high-skilled labor-saving technological innovation. An increase in the amount of offshoring shifts the iso-cost curves vertically upward, as shown in figure 1.15. The offshoring of high-skilled tasks, which we are thinking of as service activities, leads to an increase in the relative wage of skilled labor and no change in the relative wage of unskilled labor. Furthermore such offshoring will

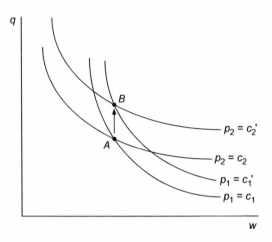

Figure 1.15
High-skilled labor-saving technical progress

reduce demand for skilled labor, at given industry outputs, as we have seen occurred in the United States during the 1990s. So the greatest contribution Grossman and Rossi-Hansberg's model, in my opinion, is that it gives us a robust way to model this service offshoring in addition to the low-skilled offshoring of the 1980s. The rich specification of offshoring costs built into the model allow for a wide array of outcomes, and go beyond the Heckscher–Ohlin structure.

Empirical Evidence

The idea the United States is now offshoring jobs that require skilled labor is not really that surprising, and probably this phenomenon has occurred from the start. Indeed *New York Times* columnist William Safire traces the earliest published use of the word "outsourcing" to an American auto executive writing in the *Journal of the Royal Society of Arts*, 1979, who said: "We are so short of professional engineers in the motor industry that we are having to outsource design work to Germany."[13] The same phenomenon appears to have occurred in Europe for some time. An early study by Magnus Blomstrom and Robert Lipsey (Blomstrom, Fors, and Lipsey 1997) has shown that Swedish multinationals establish affiliates primarily in developed countries, most likely with labor capable of performing skill-intensive tasks and this is what supports blue-collar employment at home. The smaller number of affiliates located in developing countries supports white-collar employment at home. A later study (Becker et al. 2005) is less optimistic about employment creation at home but finds that the jobs created by German and Swedish multinationals in Central and Eastern Europe more than compensates for those lost at home. Furthermore Dalia Marin (Lorentowicz et al. 2005; Marin 2005) has shown that the jobs offshored from Germany and Austria to locations in Eastern Europe are actually high-skilled jobs.

For the United States there are several studies that document the growing importance of service offshoring. Mary Amiti and Shang-Jin Wei (2005a) find that for US manufacturing, imported services grew from two-tenths of one percent of total inputs used in 1992 to three-tenths by 2000. The fact that imported services are so small does not prevent them from being important for productivity, however. Table 1.3 reports the impact of service offshoring and high-technology equipment on labor productivity in manufacturing. Over this eight-year span 12 to 17 percent of the total increase in productivity was due to service offshoring. The contribution of service imports can be compared to the contribution of high-tech equipment in manufacturing, which

Table 1.3
Impact on productivity in US manufacturing, 1992 to 2000

	Percent of total explained by each factor	
	Service offshoring	High-tech equipment
Productivity growth in manufacturing	12–17%	4–7%

Source: M. Amiti and S.-J. Wei, 2005, Service offshoring, productivity, and employment: Evidence from the United States, IMF working paper 05/238, International Monetary Fund, Washington, DC.

explains a further 4 to 7 percent of the total increase in productivity. Adding these contributions, we see that these two factors explain as much as one-quarter of the productivity growth. Since labor productivity rose by about 4 percent each year in manufacturing, we can conclude that service offshoring together with the increased use of high-tech equipment contributed as much as one percentage point of productivity growth each year, and this is economically important.

Amiti and Wei (2005a, b) do not identify a significant impact of service offshoring on employment, possibly because they work with a single aggregate of labor. But another study separates the impact of offshoring on production and nonproduction workers in US manufacturing for the 1990s (Sitchinava 2008). This study applies the two-step procedure of Feenstra and Hanson, using materials offshoring, service offshoring, as well as computer capital as potential explanatory factors. The results are summarized in table 1.4 for 1989 through 1996. While the relative wage of nonproduction workers continued to rise during this period, materials offshoring accounted for only 7 percent of that increase. Service offshoring is twice as important, contribut-

Table 1.4
Impact on the relative wage of nonproduction labor in US manufacturing, 1989 to 1996

	Percent of total increase explained by each factor		
	Materials offshoring	Service offshoring	High-technology equipment
Relative wage of nonproduction labor	7%	15%	95%

Source: N. Sitchinava, 2008, Trade, technology, and wage inequality: Evidence from U.S. manufacturing, 1989–2004, PhD dissertation, University of Oregon.
Note: Computed from the first-difference results in table 8 of Sitchinava (2008).table 1.3.

ing some 15 percent to the increase in the relative wage. But the increased use of computers (as a share of the capital stock) can account for nearly all of the rest of the rise in the relative wage.

What about employment? We have seen that relative employment of nonproduction workers fell during the 1990s, in marked contrast to the 1980s. Can we attribute that fall to routine tasks requiring skills that can be offshored? A careful study of white-collar employment in the United States (Crinò 2009), for both manufacturing and services, suggests that this is what happened in the 1990s.[14] The author finds that service offshoring raised high-skilled employment and lowered medium- and low-skilled employment. But within each skill group there was a differential response depending on whether the tasks performed are classified as routine and transportable—hence tradable. Service offshoring thus penalized those workers in the tradable occupations and benefited those in the nontradable occupations.

Factor Content of Trade Once Again

To conclude this lecture, I would like to go back to the question raised by Krugman (2008) in his recent Brookings paper: Why doesn't the factor content of trade help explain the change in wage patterns that have occurred in the United States? Some economists, for example, Leamer (2000), would say, in response, that factor contents are inadequate to predict wage changes. Others, such as Alan Deardorff (2000) and Arvind Panagariya (2000), building on the results of Deardorff and Staiger (1988), have shown that factor-content calculations can be used to predict the wage changes as compared to autarky. That result can be generalized beyond the Cobb–Douglas case to allow for CES technologies with common elasticities of substitution, or with infinitesimal changes, to more general technologies.

So I am inclined to agree with Krugman: there should be some factor content calculation for the United States that could account for the impact of increased trade on factor prices. The problem that Krugman points to is that of aggregation. We know from the detailed work on trade data by Peter Schott (2003, 2004) that a great deal of heterogeneity occurs at a very disaggregate level, for example, at the 10-digit harmonized system level, which has more than 10,000 goods; and that even *within* that level countries supply products of differing quality. If these products were all made in the United States, they would require very diverse technologies, some potentially highly labor intensive. But the factor requirements observed at the more aggregate level, often with less than 500 industries, are necessarily averages of those in the underlying activities. Working with such average factor requirements, we cannot expect to observe the underlying heterogeneity in technologies and factor use.

I would like to propose a solution to the aggregation problem that allows us to make a new factor content calculation. My solution will rely on an older technique used to analyze the HO model, due to Robert Baldwin (1971). His approach was to regress net exports across industries on their factor requirements. He finds that skilled labor has a positive coefficient in predicting net exports, while unskilled labor has a negative coefficient. I will show that univariate regressions of that type arise very naturally in the aggregation problem. The difference between the true factor contents, and those computed at an aggregate level, will depend on these Baldwin-style regressions: if there is no correlation between net exports and factor contents, then there is no aggregation problem either.

To compute the bias due to aggregation, we need, in principle, to run the Baldwin regression at a disaggregate level. Here, again we run into a problem of missing data: the net exports used as the *dependent* variable are observed at a very disaggregate level but not the factor requirements, which are used as independent variables. My solution will be to run the Baldwin regressions at a *more aggregate* level, and then apply the coefficients we obtain to the disaggregate level as well. This way we essentially "invert" the regressions and use them to infer what US factor requirements would have to be to produce highly disaggregate traded products in the United States. It will turn out that we can also keep track of the fit of the regressions, so for aggregate industries where the fit is poor, we will be able to infer correspondingly less aggregation bias in the factor content calculation.

Let me describe in detail this new approach. Suppose that there are $i = 1, \ldots, N$ goods and $j = 1, \ldots, M$ factors. The $(M \times N)$ matrix $A = [a_{ij}]'$ denotes the quantity of primary factor j used per unit output in industry i. This can be interpreted as the "direct plus indirect" factor requirements. A standard calculation of the factor content of trade for the United States is then

Factor content of trade = AT,

where the output vector for the United States is denoted by Y and the consumption vector by C so that the net export (or "trade") vector is given by $T = Y - C$.

Now consider how the measurement of the factor content of trade is affected by aggregation across industries. Suppose that the $i = 1, \ldots, N$ industries are divided into G groups, denoted by the disjoint sets I_g, each of which have N_g industries, $g = 1 \ldots, G$. The values of output, consumption and trade are then summed across industries within these groups,

$$
\bar{Y} = \begin{bmatrix} \sum_{i \in I_1} Y_i \\ \sum_{i \in I_2} Y_i \\ \vdots \\ \sum_{i \in I_G} Y_i \end{bmatrix}, \quad
\bar{C} = \begin{bmatrix} \sum_{i \in I_1} C_i \\ \sum_{i \in I_2} C_i \\ \vdots \\ \sum_{i \in I_G} C_i \end{bmatrix}, \quad \text{and} \quad
\bar{T} = \begin{bmatrix} \sum_{i \in I_1} T_i \\ \sum_{i \in I_2} T_i \\ \vdots \\ \sum_{i \in I_G} T_i \end{bmatrix}.
$$

I also need to aggregate the primary factor-requirements matrix A to obtain $\bar{A}$. I will perform this aggregation in such as way that the full-employment condition $\bar{A}\,\bar{Y} = V$ is *preserved*, where V is the vector of factor endowments for the United States. In order to preserve this condition, the factor-requirements data would need to be aggregated using the outputs of each industry as weights:

$$\bar{A} = \begin{bmatrix} \sum_{i \in I_1} \lambda_{i1} a_{i1} & \cdots & \sum_{i \in I_G} \lambda_{iG} a_{i1} \\ \sum_{i \in I_1} \lambda_{i1} a_{i2} & \cdots & \sum_{i \in I_G} \lambda_{iG} a_{i2} \\ & \vdots & \\ \sum_{i \in I_1} \lambda_{i1} a_{iM} & \cdots & \sum_{i \in I_G} \lambda_{iG} a_{iM} \end{bmatrix},$$

where $\lambda_{ig} \equiv \dfrac{Y_i}{\sum_{i \in I_g} Y_i}$, $g = 1, \ldots, G$.

The weights λ_{ig} denote the share of output of industry i within the overall output of group g. With this aggregation the full-employment condition is clearly preserved (since $\bar{A}\,\bar{Y} = AY$, which then equals endowments V). But this aggregation procedure now will *change* the calculation of the factor-content of trade:

Computed factor content of trade $= \bar{A}\,\bar{T}$.

I then can directly calculate the "aggregation bias" as follows (as proved in the appendix):

Proposition 1.2 The difference between the true factor content of trade and that obtained with aggregated data is

$$AT - \bar{A}\bar{T}$$

$$= \begin{bmatrix} \sum_{g=1}^{G} N_g \ \mathrm{cov}_g(T_i, a_{i1}) \\ \sum_{g=1}^{G} N_g \ \mathrm{cov}_g(T_i, a_{i2}) \\ \vdots \\ \sum_{g=1}^{G} N_g \ \mathrm{cov}_g(T_i, a_{iM}) \end{bmatrix} + \begin{bmatrix} \sum_{g=1}^{G} \bar{T}_g \sum_{i \in I_g} (\frac{1}{N_g} - \lambda_{ig}) a_{i1} \\ \sum_{g=1}^{G} \bar{T}_g \sum_{i \in I_g} (\frac{1}{N_g} - \lambda_{ig}) a_{i2} \\ \vdots \\ \sum_{g=1}^{G} \bar{T}_g \sum_{i \in I_g} (\frac{1}{N_g} - \lambda_{ig}) a_{iM} \end{bmatrix}.$$

Notice that the aggregation bias consists of two terms. The first depends on the covariances between the net exports in industry i and the factor requirements for industry i and factor j:

$$\text{cov}_g(T_i, a_{ij}) = \frac{1}{N_g} \sum_{i \in I_g} \left(T_i - \sum_{i \in I_g} \frac{T_i}{N_g} \right) \left(a_{ij} - \sum_{i \in I_g} \frac{a_{ij}}{N_g} \right),$$

It is immediate that this portion of the aggregation bias is *zero* when the disaggregate industries *within* each group have input requirements that are *uncorrelated* with net exports. In other words, if there is zero correlation between net exports and factor input requirements within each aggregate group, then there is no aggregation bias in computing the factor content of trade.

That zero correlation condition is unlikely to hold however, and violates the spirit of the Heckscher–Ohlin theorem, that trade is related to industry factor requirements. Certainly some correlation between net exports and factor requirements can be expected within each industry aggregate. Furthermore such a correlation will affect the second term in the aggregation bias, which is the difference between a simple and weighted average of factor requirements within each industry aggregate, multiplied by total net exports. Since the weights appearing in that formula reflect industry outputs, that second term will be nonzero when input requirements within each group are correlated with outputs, which can be expected to hold.

The challenge with implementing this formula for the aggregation bias is that the needed data, especially the factor contents, may not be observed at the same disaggregate level as the trade data. So instead, I will start with the regression equation suggested by Baldwin, run at whatever level allowed by the data: say, regressing net exports on factor requirements at the 4-digit SIC (Standard Industrial Classification) level within each 2-digit group g. I will then assume that the coefficient estimates of this regression at the 4-digit

SIC level *also hold* at a more disaggregate 10-digit HS level. At that more disaggregate level the trade information is available, which is the dependent variable in the regression. Then the estimated coefficients (from the 4-digit regression) can be used, together with the 10-digit trade data, to *infer* what the underlying factor requirements must be. That is, I essentially "invert" the regression to uncover the detailed factor requirements that are consistent with a Heckscher–Ohlin pattern of trade.

To outline this procedure more carefully, I will start with the regression of net exports on the factor requirements for each input j, for each industry group g:

$$T_i = \alpha_{gj} + \beta_{gj}\, a_{ij}, \qquad i \in I_g.$$

The estimates $\hat{\beta}_{gj}$ obtained for each factor j are given by the usual OLS formula:

$$\hat{\beta}_{gj} = \frac{\operatorname{cov}_g(T_i,\, a_{ij})}{\operatorname{var}_g(a_{ij})},$$

where the variance of the factor requirements are

$$\operatorname{var}_g(a_{ij}) = \frac{1}{N_g} \sum_{i \in I_g} \left(a_{ij} - \sum_{i \in I_g} \frac{a_{ij}}{N_g} \right)^2.$$

We can also write the R^2 of the regression for factor j as

$$R_{gj}^2 = \frac{\hat{\beta}_{gj}^2\, \operatorname{var}_g(a_{ij})}{\operatorname{var}_g(T_i)}.$$

Combining these various terms, we can write the covariance between trade and factor requirements as

$$\operatorname{cov}_g(T_i,\, a_{ij}) = \left(\frac{R_{gj}^2}{\hat{\beta}_{gj}} \right) \operatorname{var}_g(T_i).$$

In this formula for the covariance, I will use the variance of trade obtained from disaggregate, 10-digit HS trade data. But the R_{gj}^2 and $\hat{\beta}_{gj}$ coefficients are obtained from a regression at a *more aggregate level* (i.e., the 4-digit SIC industries i within each 2-digit group g). I will be assuming that those coefficients, or more precisely their ratio, apply equally well at the disaggregate level. Then this formula can be used to infer what the covariance is at the disaggregate level. This is the idea of "inverting" the Baldwin regression.

Empirical Implementation
I make use here of an input–output table for the United States for 1982, which includes 371 manufacturing industries, which are referred to as 4-digit SIC.[15] It is desirable to update this input–output table to more recent years in future work. For the initial factor-content calculation, the US net export data are concorded to the 4-digit SIC level. I can then compare the factor content of trade measured using the 4-digit data with that obtained from a calculation using 7-digit Tariff Schedule (TSUSA) level for the United States before 1989, and the 10-digit HS level after 1989.

Table 1.5 reports the results for US manufacturing in various years between 1982 and 2000. The first row for each year is simply the total usage of capital, production labor, and nonproduction labor. For example, in 1982 there were some 12 million production workers and 5 million nonproduction workers employed in manufacturing, with a ratio of 2.29 production workers for each nonproduction worker. The second row reports the content of each factor in net exports, computed using the 4-digit SIC data. In 1982 there were 229 thousand production workers imported and 95 thousand exported. If these figures are added and subtracted from the US endowments, an effective ratio of 2.37 production workers is obtained for each nonproduction worker. If instead I do the factor content calculation using the 7-digit trade data for 1982, and imputing the US factor intensities as discussed above, then for 1982 the production workers imported increases by about 50 percent and the nonproduction workers exported falls just a little. The implied effective ratio of production to nonproduction workers is then 2.39.

The increase in the effective ratio of production to nonproduction workers due to trade in 1982 is therefore quite small: slightly less than 4 percent with the 4-digit calculation, and slightly more that 4 percent with the 7-digit calculation. But manufacturing employment accounted for only about 20 percent of total US employment in the early 1980s and is less than 10 percent today. So a 4 percent effective increase in the ratio of production to nonproduction workers will not translate into a significant impact of trade on wages. But larger effects are found in later years. Looking down the final column of table 1.5, notice that the impact of trade on the effective factor endowment ratio remains less than 10 percent until 1994. In that year, there is for the first time a large impact of trade, in terms of the 10-digit calculation with imputed factor intensities. The 10-digit factor content calculation gives a net import of nearly 10 million production workers, so the ratio to nonproduction workers increases from about 2.3 to 4. In 2000 the calculation is even more dramatic, as the implied import of production workers *exceeds their employment* in US manufacturing. At this time the effective ratio of production to nonproduction workers doubles from 2.5 to 5. Even with manufacturing accounting for only 10 percent of total employment, that change in the effective ratio will have a significant impact on factor prices.

Table 1.5
Factor content of net exports for US manufacturing

Year		Capital stock ($ billion)	Production labor	Nonproduction. labor	Implied production/ nonproduction. ratio[a]
1982	Total manufacturing use	1,113	12,403	5,426	2.29
	Factor content, 4-digit data	–12	–229	95	2.37
	Factor content, 7-digit data	134	–351	79	2.39
	With 1982 input–output matrix				
1985	Total manufacturing use	1,151	12,171	5,332	2.28
	Factor content, 4-digit data	–104	–1,324	–322	2.39
	Factor content, 7-digit data	–26	–776	–306	2.30
1988	Total manufacturing use	1,116	12,404	5,514	2.25
	Factor content, 4-digit data	–92	–1,420	–349	2.36
	Factor content, 7-digit data	–288	–1,385	–136	2.44
1991	Total manufacturing use	1,204	11,514	5,279	2.18
	Factor content, 4-digit data	–34	–844	–130	2.28
	Factor content, 10-digit data	–123	–861	–104	2.30
1994	Total manufacturing use	1,285	11,946	5,139	2.32
	Factor content, 4-digit data	–73	–1,252	–304	2.42
	Factor content, 10-digit data	–77	–9,447	–277	3.95

Table 1.5
(continued)

Year		Capital stock ($ billion)	Production labor	Nonpro- duction. labor	Implied production/ nonproduction. ratio[a]
1997[b]	Total manu- facturing use	na	12,065	4,740	2.55
	Factor content, 4-digit data	−56	−1,133	−201	2.67
	Factor content, 10-digit data	−310	−1,840	−240	2.79
2000[b]	Total manu- facturing use	na	11,944	4,708	2.54
	Factor content, 4-digit data	−133	−2,002	−515	2.54
	Factor content, 10-digit data	94	−13,883	−468	4.99

a. For total direct and indirect usage, this is the ratio of production to non-production labor. For the factor content calculations, we reverse the sign (i.e., take the factor content of imports), add the imported production and nonproduction labor to the total usage, and then take the ratio.
b. Calculations for 1997 and 2000 use the same factor requirements as in 1994, but update the trade data.

As I have just shown, a factor content calculation can potentially give us a large impact of trade on factor prices, once we impute the factor intensities corresponding to disaggregate trade flows. Additional work is needed to confirm this result for the United States, since I have made simplifying assumptions in the calculations: the estimates in table 1.5 use an input–output matrix from 1982, and the final years all use domestic shipments data from 1994. In addition I have not experimented with constraining the Baldwin-style regressions to be stable across years, which might explain why the 10-digit results for 1997 give only a small impact of factor contents on the implied effective factor ratio, unlike what was found for 1994 and 2000. And of course, it is most important to check my assumption that the coefficients of the Baldwin-style regression run at the 4-digit SIC level can actually be applied at more disaggregate levels. But even with all these considerations, the preliminary results are promising enough to convince us that headway can be made on the aggregation problem in factor content calculations. In future work we can expect to find more profound impacts of offshoring as measured by the factor content of trade.

Notes

1. Both the narrow and more common definitions are provided in the OECD Glossary of Statistical Terms; see http://stats.oecd.org/glossary/detail.asp?ID=6271. Bhagwati, Panagariya and Srinivasan (2004) focus on foreign outsourcing defined as "offshore trade in arm's length services," reflecting the growing importance of services trade. I will distinguish between materials offshoring and services offshoring later in this lecture.

2. J. Bhagwati (2007, p. 11).

3. See Sachs and Schatz (1994, 1998), as well as Krueger (1997).

4. Nevertheless, Leamer still refers to the 1970s as the Stolper–Samuelson decade, in the sense that that it is changes in product prices, and not total factor productivity, that are principally responsible for the change in wages.

5. Leamer (1994, p. 14) recognizes that if technological change leads to induced changes in product prices, then the implied change in wages are impacted. He writes: "One last point. These derivatives for studying technological changes take prices as given, but, if the technological improvement is nonneutral, nonproprietary and worldwide, the increased relative supply of the technologically advantaged products is likely to be accompanied by offsetting reductions in their relative prices. An estimate of the full effect of technological change on wages would of course have to allow for these induced price changes." See also Leamer (1998, p. 182): "Thus, to do the job right, we really need a complete worldwide, general equilibrium model, input-output model. We need this to deal with second-order effects, to deal with pass-through rates, and also to determine sectoral-biased price changes induced by factor-biased technological change."

6. Feenstra and Hanson (1999) treat the structural variables as exogenous, but that is arguably not the case. More recent work by Voigtlaender (2008) shows how instruments for offshoring and high-technology equipment can be constructed by using data on neighboring sectors.

7. Doms, Dunne, and Troske (1997) argue that *current* computer investment is correlated with *past* skill upgrading, suggesting that computer investment is correlated with unobserved feature of firms or industries that lead them to shift toward more skilled labor. In that case computer investment does not "cause" skill up-grading.

8. L. Uchitell, To mend the flaws in trade, *New York Times*, January 30, 2007, pp. C1–C7.

9. Other labor economists disagree, however, and argue that the changing patterns from the 1980s to the 1990s suggest that skill-biased technological change was not the right explanation in the first place. Examples of this so-called revisionist school of thought are Card and DiNardo (2002) and Lemieux (2006).

10. Economics focus, the great unbundling: Does economics need a new theory of offshoring? *The Economist*, January 18, 2007.

11. Recall that Xu (2001) modeled technical progress as a_j and b_j in the cost function $c_j(a_jw, b_jq)$. A drop in a_j is analogous to the drop in β in the offshoring model, which increases the relative demand for high-skilled labor if and only if $\sigma_j < 1$.

12. Analogously, Kohler (2001) has shown that the fragmentation results of Arndt (1997) no longer hold when capital is sector-specific, so there are more factors than goods. See also Kohler (2004).

13. W. Safire, On language, *New York Times Magazine*, March 21, 2004, p. 30.

14. Crinò (2007) finds that service offshoring also raises the demand for high-skilled labor in Western Europe.

15. Following Trefler and Zhu (2000), we subtract *imported* intermediate inputs from this matrix before using it as B. The trade and direct factor requirements are concorded with those of the 371 industries, with three factors of production (capital, production labor, and nonproduction labor). Having obtained the director factor requirements D (3×371), and the input–output matrix B (371×371), we compute the total factor requirements (direct plus indirect) as $A = D(I - B)^{-1}$. See Feenstra and Hanson (2000).

Lecture 2: Macroeconomic Implications

In lecture 1, I discussed in depth the microeconomic structure of trade models with offshoring. Now I will shift attention to macroeconomic implications, of which three come to mind immediately: business cycle volatility, price determination, and productivity. We will begin with business cycle volatility. The model discussed in lecture 1, whereby firms choose the least-cost country for each stage of the production process, allows for the rapid movement of activities across countries in response to wage movements. This is an example of what Jagdish Bhagwati (1997) calls "kaleidoscopic comparative advantage." Writing in the *Financial Times*, he explains that this phenomenon "leads to volatility of jobs, as you have an advantage today and can lose it tomorrow"[1] I will argue that such rapid movement has been seen in the experience of the Mexican economy, and especially the *maquiladora* sector, in which are the Mexican firms located just south of the US border. That sector of the economy displays more volatility than overall for Mexican manufacturing, and also more volatility than those industries in the United States. This amplified volatility is not a coincidence, and in fact, it follows from the structure of the models that were discussed in lecture 1.

Second, we will turn attention to the nominal side of the economy, to prices and exchange rates. This is a topic that was discussed in last year's Ohlin lecture by Ken Rogoff.[2] The impact of offshoring, or globalization more generally, on nominal variables is inherently controversial. As Milton Friedman (1974) famously said: "Inflation is always and everywhere a monetary phenomena . . . ," which does not seem to leave much room for international trade to enter the equation. But researchers are now asking whether increased globalization is responsible for least some of the movements in prices and exchange rates that have been observed in recent years.

Of particular interest is the question of whether the pass-through of nominal exchange rate to import prices, and ultimately to domestic prices, differs today than that in past decades. I will show how the pass-through of the dollar exchange rate to US import prices depends on the share of imports coming from China, a leading location for offshoring. Demonstrating that result will require changing one assumption often used in the monopolistic competition model, and that is the assumption of CES preferences. So I will introduce instead translog preferences that allow the markups of firms to vary due to market pressures: these changing markups will end up having macroeconomic effects on prices.[3]

Besides the exchange rate, aggregate prices can be affected by offshoring through its impact on productivity. This is an issue that has received much attention recently in Washington, DC, with various statistical agencies trying to update their procedures to deal with this new form of international trade. I will examine how offshoring, or globalization more generally, has affected productivity growth in the United States. While there can be a direct, positive impact of trade on productivity (as in Melitz 2003), my focus will be on a indirect impact due to the mismeasurement of tradable goods prices. I will argue that a portion of the productivity speedup in the United States during the latter half of the 1990s was actually due improvements in the terms of trade, that are incorrectly attributed to productivity.[4] Consumers benefit in any case, but it is important to identify the source of these gains as due to international trade.

Business Cycle Volatility

Let us begin with the connection between offshoring and volatility. The idea that openness to trade might amplify the volatility of an economy is hardly new, and has been studied empirically for some time. Early work by William Easterly and Joseph Stiglitz (Easterly, Islam, and Stiglitz 2000) established that increased openness contributed to aggregate volatility across a wide range of countries. That conclusion has now been re-examined at a sectoral level (Di Giovanni and Levchenko 2009) who find that there are two offsetting effects: that sectors more open to international trade are more volatile, but that they are also less correlated with the rest of the economy. On net, the evidence still suggests that sectoral openness leads to increased aggregate volatility, but this effect is stronger for developing economies. If we add the firm dimension, as done by Claudia Buch for Germany (Buch, Döpke, and Strotmann 2007), then we find instead that exporting leads to less firm-level volatility.

With this range of empirical results, we cannot help but ask: what is the model? My own contribution in this area, with Paul Bergin and Gordon Hanson, is to construct a model that is very closely related to the offshoring literature but introduces demand and supply shocks (Bergin, Feenstra, and

Hanson 2007, 2009a, b). It turns out that only demand shocks are important, for reasons that I will explain. Furthermore it turns out the demand shocks have differential impacts on the home country where offshoring originates, and the foreign country where the offshoring takes place. Essentially offshoring allows the home country to export its business cycle fluctuations so that volatility is amplified abroad. The idea that the parallel movements of business cycles across countries will depend on whether we are looking at North–North versus North–South trade, and also depend on the vertical linkages between countries, has been confirmed in recent empirical work (Burstein, Kurz, and Tesar 2008; Giovanni and Levchenko 2009). Linda Tesar has recently extended that work to study the synchronization of business cycles across Eastern and Western Europe (Tesar 2008).

Model of Offshoring
Let me briefly outline the theoretical model that I have in mind. To simplify the offshoring model from lecture 1, suppose that there is a single factor of production—labor. There is again a continuum of activities, which we arrange in increasing order of US or home country comparative advantage. Then, just like the Ricardian model with a continuum of goods, we obtain a downward-sloping schedule between relative labor requirements at home and abroad:

$$A(z) \equiv \frac{a(z)}{a^*(z)} = \exp(bz + c), \qquad b < 0,$$

where the exponential form for this schedule will simplify our calculations below.

The intersection between the relative labor requirements $A(z)$ and the relative wage determines the borderline activity that can be done in either country, shown in figure 2.1. The

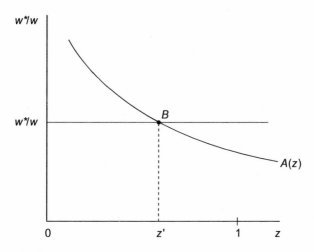

Figure 2.1
Equilibrium with offshoring

home country will perform those activities above z', while
the foreign country will perform those activities below z'.
These activities are treated like intermediate inputs, which
are produced in multiple varieties under monopolistic
competition, with CES preferences and N firms producing
each good z. These inputs are then combined into a final,
multinational good using a symmetric Cobb–Douglas
function.

We close the model by adding country-specific homogeneous goods that are produced in each country and also
traded. The key results can be seen by focusing on labor
demand for the multinational good. Denote world demand
by $\bar{D}_M \equiv [D_M + D_M^*(1-n)/n]$, where n is a parameter reflecting
the size of the home country relative to the foreign country.
The labor earnings at home from production of the activities
above z' are just

$$wL_M = \bar{D}_M (1 - z') \left(\frac{\sigma - 1}{\sigma} \right),$$

where σ is the elasticity of substitution between varieties of good z. These labor earnings include both the fixed costs and variables costs used in production. It will be convenient to make use of the equilibrium condition to rewrite the employment in the offshored good at home as

$$\frac{w^*}{w} = A(z') \Rightarrow L_M = \left(\frac{\bar{D}_M}{w^*} \right)(1 - z')A(z')\left(\frac{\sigma - 1}{\sigma} \right).$$

Likewise employment in the offshored good in the foreign country is simply

$$L_M^* = \left(\frac{\bar{D}_M}{w^*} \right)(z')\left(\frac{n}{n-1} \right)\left(\frac{\sigma - 1}{\sigma} \right).$$

Taking the logs and variance of these two employment equations, we obtain the following:

$$\text{var}(\ln L_M) = \text{var}\left[\ln\left(\frac{\bar{D}_M}{w^*} \right) \right] + \left[\frac{1}{1 - \bar{z}'} - b \right]^2$$
$$\times \text{var}(z') - 2\left[\frac{1}{1 - \bar{z}'} - b \right]\text{cov}\left[z', \ln\left(\frac{\bar{D}_M}{w^*} \right) \right]$$

and

$$\text{var}(\ln L_{Mt}^*) = \text{var}\left[\ln\left(\frac{\bar{D}_M}{w^*} \right) \right] + \frac{\text{var}(z')}{(\bar{z}')^2} + \frac{2}{\bar{z}'}\text{cov}\left[z', \ln\left(\frac{\bar{D}_M}{w^*} \right) \right],$$

where $\bar{z}'$ denotes the mean level of production activities in Mexico.

From these expressions we can see that the variance of employment in each country depends on three factors: first, on the variance of world demand relative to the foreign wage; second, on the variance of the offshoring margin z', which is measured *relative to* an 'adjusted' size of the offshoring sector, $\{[1/(1-\bar{z}')]-b\}$ at home and $(1/\bar{z}')$ abroad; and third, on the covariance between z' and world demand. The first term, which is the variance of world demand relative to the foreign wage, enters identically in both expressions, so it does not lead to any asymmetric effect across countries. The second term, which is the variance of the offshoring margin z', has a bigger impact in the foreign country when the range of activities done there is small. This just reflects the idea that the percentage impact of any given demand fluctuations on employment will be greater if the economy is smaller. Finally, the covariance between the offshoring margin z' and world demand enters with opposite signs in the two countries. Provided this covariance is positive, it *lowers* the variance of employment at home but *amplifies it abroad*.

We expect that this covariance is in fact positive from the structure of the model. World demand for the offshored good will be most highly correlated with home, or US demand, since it is the larger economy. An increase in US demand will raise US relative wages, resulting in a shift in the offshoring margin from z' to z^* in figure 2.2. So offshoring activities get shifted to Mexico at the same time as demand is booming, thereby amplifying the volatility of employment there. On the other hand, the impact of the demand shock in the United States is offset by shifting production abroad. So there is an asymmetric impact of demand shocks on the two countries.

The focus on demand shocks goes against the conventional practice in real business cycle models of focusing on productivity shocks. The reason that such supply-side shocks have been ignored so far is that they have only limited effects in

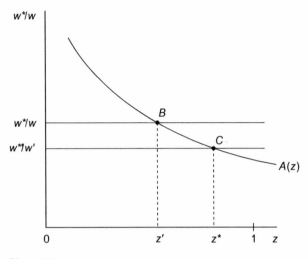

Figure 2.2
Increase in offshoring due to rise in home wage

the model. This result follows from my discussion in lecture 1 of Krugman's (2000) two-country, two-good model with Cobb–Douglas preferences. He showed that Hicks-neutral productivity shocks have no impact on employment: the fall in price and increase in demand following a rise in productivity just offsets the potential decline in employment. The model presented here actually has three goods, with a homogeneous good exported by each country and also the offshored good. But the same result as in Krugman's model will hold provided that productivity shocks in the offshoring sector are transmitted instantaneously between countries so that there is no shift in the $A(z)$ schedule. In this offshoring model we can conclude that demand shocks, and not productivity shocks, are the chief source of international transmission of business cycles.

Empirical Evidence

Let us turn now to the evidence for the United States and Mexico. To avoid the period of the peso crisis in 1994 to 1995, we focus the analysis on the period 1996 to 2005. Figure 2.3 plots the production-worker employment for the four main offshoring industries, which are apparel, electronic materials, electronic machinery, and transport equipment. In each industry, employment in Mexico (shown by the dashed line) is substantially more volatile than in the United States. That perception is reinforced by looking at the standard deviations of log employment in US manufacturing industries and the corresponding maquiladora plants in Mexico. Table 2.1 shows the standard deviations for the production-worker employment in Mexican and US industries, and in the bottom rows, the ratio of Mexico to the United States. On average, the standard deviation of Mexican employment is about twice as high as that in the United States in each industry, but it is smaller than for US overall manufacturing.

One simple explanation for volatility to be higher in the Mexican offshoring industries is that these industries are smaller than US industries; with idiosyncratic shocks across plants, US employment may be smoothing out shocks. The size differences between the Mexican and US industries are investigated in table 2.2 where from the employment listed for each industry we see that in two of the four industries US employment is indeed much larger. We can deal better with these size disparities by focusing on particular US states. The vast majority of maquiladoras in Mexico are located in Mexican border cities, and many are linked to production operations on the US side of the border (Feenstra, Hanson, and Swenson 2000) in California and Texas.

So we next compare Mexican industries to their counterparts in California and Texas. Table 2.2 shows that employ-

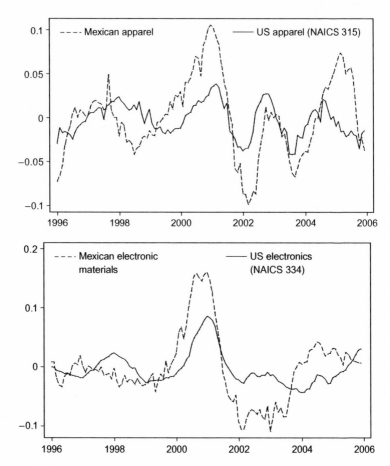

Figure 2.3
Employment for production workers in Mexican and US offshoring industries (log values, seasonally adjusted and HP filtered). Source: Bergin, Feenstra, and Hanson (2007, 2009a).

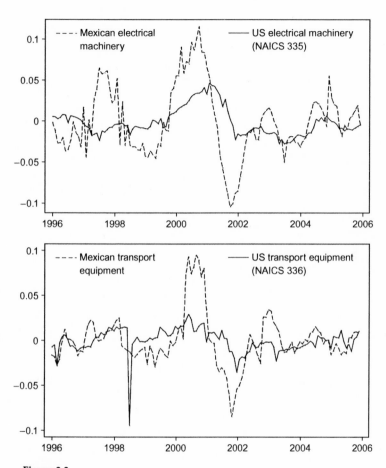

Figure 2.3
(continued)

Table 2.1
Relative volatility in Mexican and US offshoring industries: Production-worker employment

Standard deviations, employment	Apparel	Electrical machinery	Computer and electronics	Transport equipment	Average
$\sigma(L_i^*)$ (Mexican offshoring industry)	4.52	4.34	5.95	2.96	4.44
$\sigma(L_i)$ (US offshoring industry)	1.89	1.79	3.06	1.42	2.04
$\sigma(L^*)$ (Mexican aggregate manufacturing)	0.89	0.89	0.89	0.89	0.89
$\sigma(L)$ (US aggregate manufacturing)	1.15	1.15	1.15	1.15	1.15
$\sigma(L_i^*)/\sigma(L_i)$	2.39	2.42	1.94	2.08	2.21
$\sigma(L^*)/\sigma(L)$	0.77	0.77	0.77	0.77	0.77

Source: Bergin, Feenstra, and Hanson (2007, 2009a).
Notes: Standard deviations (in percent) are for the production-worker employment in specific Mexican and US offshoring industries, and in Mexican and US aggregate manufacturing, and the ratios of these standard deviations. Each series is in log values, seasonally adjusted, and HP filtered. Data are monthly from 1996 through 2005.

ment in offshoring industries of California and Texas is similar in scale to that of Mexican industries. Table 2.3 shows that standard deviations and their ratios based on state employment data are broadly similar to those obtained for national data: the four offshoring industries are somewhat less than twice as volatile in Mexico as compared to California and Texas, whereas overall Mexican manufacturing employment is less volatile than that in either state. So even after correcting for size differences, we still obtain more industry-level volatility in the Mexican maquiladora.

The theoretical model just described implies that changes in employment by offshoring industries are driven in part

Table 2.2
Size of offshoring industries in Mexico and the United States

| NAICS | Industry | Thousands of employees (mean 2000–2005) | | | |
		Mexico	United States	Texas	California
	All maquiladoras (Mexico)	1,151.00	—	—	—
	All manufacturing (United States)	—	15,336.70	955.5	1,649.00
315	Apparel	230.8	356.9	—	97.4
334	Computer and electronics	265.6	1,512.30	132.9	366.6
335	Electrical machinery	100.2	497.5	20.0	38.5
336	Transport equipment	240.7	1,855.80	85.2	137.5

Source: US Bureau of Economic Analysis, Regional Economic Information System, http://www.bea.gov/bea/regional/reis/; Mexico's National Institute for Statistics, Geography, and Informatics (INEGI), http://www.bea.gov/bea/regional/reis/. As cited in Bergin, Feenstra, and Hanson (2007, 2009a).

by adjustment at the extensive margin. If such a mechanism is at work, we should see considerable entry and exit among the assembly plants in Mexico that produce intermediate goods and services for US industry. There is abundant anecdotal evidence of such plant turnover from firms such as Delphi, a large US manufacturer of auto parts. It has opened and closed assembly plants in Mexico during a period of expansion and contraction. To see whether there is more formal evidence of adjustment at the extensive margin, we can look at employment data. Let us start with an identity linking industry employment to the employment per plant and the number of plants:

$$E_{it} \equiv N_{it} \times \frac{E_{it}}{N_{it}} \equiv \frac{E_{it}}{E_t} \times E_t,$$

Table 2.3
Relative volatility in Mexican and US offshoring industries: Total employment at the US state level

	Apparel	Electrical machinery	Computer and electronics	Transport equipment	Average
California					
$\sigma(L_i^*)$ (Mexican offshoring industry)	4.48	4.11	5.50	2.73	4.21
$\sigma(L_i)$ (US offshoring industry)	2.25	2.35	2.62	1.31	2.13
$\sigma(L^*)$ (Mexican aggregate manufacturing)	0.77	0.77	0.77	0.77	0.77
$\sigma(L)$ (US aggregate manufacturing)	1.40	1.40	1.40	1.40	1.40
$\sigma(L_i^*)/\sigma(L_i)$	1.99	1.75	2.10	2.08	1.98
$\sigma(L^*)/\sigma(L)$	0.55	0.55	0.55	0.55	0.55
Texas					
$\sigma(L_i^*)$ (Mexican offshoring industry)	4.48	4.11	5.50	2.73	3.09
$\sigma(L_i)$ (US offshoring industry)	na	2.48	3.12	1.66	2.42
$\sigma(L^*)$ (Mexican aggregate manufacturing)	0.77	0.77	0.77	0.77	0.77
$\sigma(L)$ (US aggregate manufacturing)	1.16	1.16	1.16	1.16	1.16
$\sigma(L_i^*)/\sigma(L_i)$	na	1.66	1.76	1.64	1.69
$\sigma(L^*)/\sigma(L)$	na	0.66	0.66	0.66	0.66

Source: Bergin, Feenstra, and Hanson (2007, 2009a).
Note: "na" indicates this industry is not available for that state.

where E_{it} is employment in industry i at time t, N_{it} is the number of plants in industry i at t, and E_t is aggregate employment in Mexico at t. From this identity we specify two regressions:

$$\ln N_{it} = \alpha_0 + \alpha_1 \ln \frac{E_{it}}{E_t} + \alpha_2 E_t + \varepsilon_{it}$$

and

$$\ln \frac{E_{it}}{N_{it}} = \beta_0 + \beta_1 \ln \frac{E_{it}}{E_t} + \beta_2 E_t - \varepsilon_{it}.$$

Because we started with an identity, the coefficients will sum to zero or unity across these regressions, $\alpha_0 + \beta_0 = 0$, $\alpha_1 + \beta_1 = 1$, and $\alpha_2 + \beta_2 = 1$.

In table 2.4 we report the result from these regressions using data for the employment and number of firms in the maquiladora industries. In the first column the estimates show that in response to an increase in the share of aggregate employment in an offshoring industry, over one-third of adjustment in industry employment occurs at the extensive margin, in the number of plants. Further, in response to an increase in aggregate employment, nearly one-half of adjustment in industry employment occurs at the extensive margin. So it appears that plant entry and exit is an important channel by which the maquiladora industry adjusts to aggregate shocks.

Summing up, we have shown that the variance of employment in Mexico's maquiladora industries exceeds that in the corresponding industries in the United States, with some of that volatility due to adjustment at the extensive margin. These observations fit the theoretical model described above, where home demand shocks have an amplified impact on

Table 2.4
Adjustment in the maquiladora industry: Extensive margins

	Dependent variables	
	Number of plants	Employment per plant
Industry share of	0.38	0.62
Aggregate employment	(0.16)	(0.16)
Aggregate employment	0.49	0.51
	(0.05)	(0.05)
R^2	0.30	0.51
N	480	480

Source: Bergin, Feenstra, and Hanson (2009a).
Notes: Regressionsof the number of plants (column 1) and employment per plant (column 2) are on total Mexican manufacturing employment and the industry share of manufacturing employment. The sample is the four offshoring industries in Mexico, with data at a monthly frequency from 1996:1 to 2005:12. All variables are in logs, expressed in real terms, de-seasonalized, and HP filtered. All regressions include controls for industry fixed effects, which are not shown. Standard errors (clustered by industry) are in parentheses.

the foreign country. In Bergin, Feenstra, and Hanson (2009b), we simulate the same model using home and foreign demand and productivity shocks, each calibrated to US and Mexican values. We confirm that US demand shocks are the principal cause of the extra volatility in the Mexican maquiladora industries.

That fact that the maquiladora industries are more volatile means that the United States is essentially exporting some of its business cycle, or more precisely, exporting the cyclical fluctuations due to demand shocks. In addition offshoring increases the size of cross-country correlations in employment, which are all positive in the data and the simulations. That result is consistent with the finding of Linda Tesar (2008) for offshoring between Western and Eastern Europe.

She argues that an increase in trade between these regions, due to the recent expansion of the European Union or a future expansion of the euro zone, will lead to even greater output correlation between these economies. So this feature of offshoring models, which has only begun to be explored, is of interest for both policy and theoretical reasons.

Prices and Exchange Rates

Let us turn now to a second macroeconomic implication of offshoring, or of globalization more generally, and that is the impact on prices and exchange rates. The fact that inflation has moderated in many countries over the past two decades, while globalization has increased, has naturally led analysts to wonder whether one has caused the other. Officials in Japan have stated most clearly that they believe the deflation there has been imported from China. Writing in the *Financial Times* in 2002, the Vice Minister and Deputy Vice Minister for International Affairs at the Japanese Ministry of Finance said,[5]

The entry of emerging market economies—such as China and other East Asian nations—into the global trading system is a powerful additional deflationary force. Their combined supply capacity has been exerting downward pressure on the prices of goods in industrialized economies . . . . China is exporting deflation and its effects are not limited to neighboring Hong Kong and Taiwan.

Evidence for the United States is summarized in a recent paper by Rick Mishkin (Mishkin 2009). He strikes a cautionary note on the belief that globalization has affected inflation, quoting the maxim of Milton Friedman (1974). That idea has been stated most forcefully in recent times by Larry Ball (2006), who describes the import price as a *relative* price in the economy, and any decline in that price will by definition be matched by an increase in some other relative price. So he claims there is no connection whatsoever between import prices and inflation. That iron-clad rule is too strong for me, and perhaps for Mishkin too, who cites research showing that import competition from China has played some role in lowering import prices, and therefore consumer prices, in the United States and the OECD more generally.[6] But at the same time, the demand from China for resources has also raised commodity prices, so the net impact on global prices is likely to be small.

I would like to address the question of what role China might have played in lowering US prices by asking once again: what is the model? The common argument for why China can make a difference relies on its impact on the markups charged by firms. That is a difficult argument to assess because our basic model of monopolistic competition, using CES demand, has constant markups. So to make any headway, we need to go beyond the CES case and allow for preferences where the elasticity changes with the number of competing firms. A class of preferences that allows for such variable markups is the translog expenditure function.[7] The translog unit-expenditure function for a consumer is written as

$$\ln e(p) \ = \ \alpha_0 + \sum_{i=1}^{\bar{N}} \alpha_i \ln p_i + \frac{1}{2} \sum_{i=1}^{\bar{N}} \sum_{j=1}^{\bar{N}} \gamma_{ij} \ln p_i \ln p_j,$$

where, without loss of generality, we impose the symmetry restriction that $\gamma_{ij} = \gamma_{ji}$. The parameter $\bar{N}$ is the maximum number of possible products, but many of these might not be produced: the prices used for products not available should equal their reservation prices (where demand is zero).

Notice that in the CES case the reservation prices are infinite, so these prices drop out of the CES expenditure function (where the infinite prices are raised to a negative power). But in the translog case we need to explicitly solve for the reservation prices.

For the translog expenditure function to be homogeneous of degree one, we need to impose the conditions

$$\sum_{i=1}^{\tilde{N}} \alpha_i = 1 \quad \text{and} \quad \sum_{i=1}^{\tilde{N}} \gamma_{ij} = 0.$$

I will further impose a strong form of symmetry on the γ_{ij} coefficients, which is

$$\gamma_{ii} = -\gamma\left(\frac{\tilde{N}-1}{\tilde{N}}\right) \quad \text{and} \quad \gamma_{ij} = \frac{\gamma}{\tilde{N}} \quad \text{for } i \neq j,$$

with $i, j = 1, \ldots, \tilde{N}$.

That is, we require that the Γ matrix have the same negative value on the diagonal, and the same positive value on the off-diagonal terms, with the rows and columns summing to zero as needed for the expenditure function to be homogeneous of degree one. Notice that it does no harm to make these parameters depend on $\tilde{N}$, which is just a fixed maximum number.

Now suppose that some of the varieties are not available, so the prices faced by the consumer equal his or her reservation prices. Then using these strong symmetry restrictions, we can solve for the reservation prices for goods not available, substitute these back into the expenditure function, and obtain a reduced-form expenditure function that is very convenient to work with. In particular, this reduced-form expenditure function remains valid even as the number of available products—which we denote by N—varies. The following result shows that the reduced form expenditure function is still a symmetric translog:

Proposition 2.1 (Feenstra 2003; Bergin and Feenstra 2009)
Suppose that the strong symmetry restrictions, with $\gamma > 0$, are imposed on the expenditure function. In addition suppose that only the goods $i = 1, \ldots, N$ are available, so that the reservation prices for $j = N + 1, \ldots, \tilde{N}$ are used. Then the expenditure function becomes

$$\ln e(p) = a_0 + \sum_{i=1}^{N} a_i \ln p_i + \frac{1}{2} \sum_{i=1}^{N} \sum_{j=1}^{N} c_{ij} \ln p_i \ln p_j,$$

where

$$c_{ii} = -\frac{\gamma(N-1)}{N} \quad \text{and} \quad c_{ij} = \frac{\gamma}{N} \quad \text{for } i \neq j, \text{ with } i, j = 1, \ldots, N,$$

and where

$$a_i = a_i + \frac{1}{N}\left(1 - \sum_{i=1}^{N} a_i\right) \quad \text{for } i = 1, \ldots, N,$$

$$a_0 = \alpha_0 + \left(\frac{1}{2\gamma}\right)\left\{\sum_{i=N+1}^{\tilde{N}} \alpha_i^2 + \left(\frac{1}{N}\right)\left(\sum_{i=N+1}^{\tilde{N}} \alpha_i\right)^2\right\}.$$

Notice that this reduced form expenditure function looks like a conventional translog function, but now defined over the *available* goods $i = 1, \ldots, N$, while the strong symmetry restrictions on γ_{ij} continue to hold on the coefficients c_{ij}, but using N rather than $\tilde{N}$. To interpret the coefficient a_i, they imply each of the coefficients α_i is increased by the same amount to ensure that the coefficients a_i sum to unity over the available goods $I = 1, \ldots, N$. Finally, the term a_0 incorporates the coefficients α_i of the unavailable products. If the number of available products N rises, then a_0 falls, indicating a welfare gain from increasing variety.

By this proposition, we can work with the reduced-form expenditure function, knowing that the reservation prices for unavailable goods are being solved for in the background. We can differentiate the unit-expenditure function to obtain the expenditure shares

$$s_i = a_i + \sum_{j=1}^{N} c_{ij} \ln p_j.$$

The elasticity of demand is obtained by differentiating these shares,

$$\eta_i = 1 - \frac{\partial \ln s_i}{\partial \ln p_i} = 1 - \frac{c_{ii}}{s_i} = 1 + \frac{\gamma(N-1)}{s_i N}.$$

We see that the elasticity of demand is inversely related to the market share of each firm: as the market share approaches zero, then the elasticity is infinite. With equal-sized firms charging the same prices, the market share is $s_i = 1/N$, and in that case the elasticity is simplified as

$$s_i = \frac{1}{N} \Rightarrow \eta_i = 1 + \gamma(N-1),$$

which is linearly related to the number of firms in the market. If we also chose $\gamma = 1$, which is an allowable choice for the translog parameter, then we find that the elasticity of demand equals the number of firms in the market, $\eta_i = N$.

These observations on the elasticity carry over to the markups charged by firms. The optimal prices under monopolistic competition are

$$p_i = w_i \left(\frac{\eta_i}{\eta_i - 1} \right) = w_i \left(1 + \frac{s_i N}{\gamma(N-1)} \right),$$

so the markups are increasing in each firm's market share. As the shares approach zero, the firms approach the perfectly competitive equilibrium, and when there are fewer firm, then the markups correspondingly rise.

Competition between China and Mexico in the US Market
Let us now use this framework to return to the question of how a growing China can impact prices in the United States. The observation made by many researchers at the Federal Reserve Bank in the United States is that as the dollar has depreciated in recent years, the impact on import prices has been less than expected: instead of rising by 50 percent of the appreciation in foreign currencies, import prices have risen by only 20 percent, so pass-through has declined from 0.5 in the 1980s to something like 0.2 today. This decline in the pass-through of the exchange rate to import prices is some-times attributed to the presence of China in many markets.[8] It can be reasoned the China's presence, together with its essentially fixed exchange rate to the dollar, limits the increase in prices that might occur from flexible rate countries such as Mexico. So it is really the interaction of fixed and floating rate countries, in a model with endogenous markups, that has led to the declining pass-through of exchange rates to import prices.

We can make this argument formally by using the translog preferences together with a three country model: Mexico, denoted by x; China, denoted by y; and the United States, denoted by z. We abstract from many of the features of our earlier offshoring model, including the continuum of inter-mediate inputs.We simply assume instead that Mexico and China compete for sales in the United States, which is real-istic enough. We model the US demand for the products of these two countries as following the translog preferences, and for simplicity, suppose that the United States produces a separate homogeneous good. Then with a depreciation of the dollar, the question is how the Mexican and Chinese firms respond.

We assume that Mexican firms are symmetric, facing marginal cost of w_x and charging the prices of p_x in pesos. Their dollar prices are then $e_x p_x$, where e_x is the floating \$/peso exchange rate. Likewise Chinese firms are symmetric and face marginal costs of w_y while charging the prices p_y in yuan, so their dollar prices are $\overline{e}_y p_y$, where $\overline{e}_y$ is the fixed \$/yuan exchange rate. From the translog share equations, the market shares of each Mexican and Chinese firm in the United States are given by

$$s_x = a_x - \frac{\gamma N_y}{N}\left[\ln(e_x p_x) - \ln(\overline{e}_y p_y)\right],$$

$$s_y = a_y - \frac{\gamma N_x}{N}\left[\ln(\overline{e}_y p_y) - \ln(e_x p_x)\right],$$

where N_x or N_y denotes the number of Mexican or Chinese varieties sold in the US market, with $N_x + N_y = N$. We will assume that there is a US taste bias in favor of products from Mexico, meaning that

$$\alpha_x > \alpha_y \Leftrightarrow a_x > a_y.$$

This assumption is strongly supported by results from gravity equations, for example, that give a bias in favor of countries sharing a border with the importer.

The pricing equation for each firm gives us their optimal prices as a function of market shares and, by the log approximation, $\ln[1 + s_i N/\gamma(N-1)] \approx s_i N/\gamma(N-1)$, which is valid for small shares. So we can write the optimal prices as

$$\ln p_x \approx \ln w_x + \frac{a_x N}{\gamma(N-1)} - \frac{N_y}{N-1}\left[\ln(e_x p_x) - \ln(\overline{e}_y p_y)\right],$$

$$\ln p_y \approx \ln w_y + \frac{a_y N}{\gamma(N-1)} - \frac{N_x}{N-1}\left[\ln(\overline{e}_y p_y) - \ln(e_x p_x)\right].$$

These are two equations to solve for the two prices—of Mexican and Chinese goods—depending on their marginal costs. We can solve this system for the dollar prices:

$$\ln(e_x p_x) = \frac{1}{\gamma(N-1)} + \ln(e_x w_x) + \frac{N_y}{(2N-1)}\frac{A}{\gamma}$$

and

$$\ln(\overline{e}_y p_y) = \frac{1}{\gamma(N-1)} + \ln(\overline{e}_y w_y) - \frac{N_x}{(2N-1)}\frac{A}{\gamma},$$

where the parameter A reflects the bias in favor of Mexican firms:

$$A \equiv (\alpha_x - \alpha_y) - \gamma[\ln(e_x w_x) - \ln(\overline{e}_y w_y)].$$

Notice that this parameter depends, in part, on an assumed taste bias in favor of Mexican compared to Chinese products, $\alpha_x > \alpha_y$, and also depends on the marginal costs in the two locations, which we assume does not overturn the initial bias favoring Mexico. That is, we will assume that $A > 0$.

Holding wages fixed, the effect of a dollar depreciation on the dollar prices of Mexican and Chinese goods can be easily solved as

$$\frac{d\ln(e_x p_x)}{d\ln e_x} = 1 - \frac{N_y}{2N-1} > 0$$

and

$$\frac{d\ln(\overline{e}_y p_y)}{d\ln e_x} = \frac{N_x}{2N-1} > 0.$$

We see from the first equation that the dollar depreciation raises the dollar price of Mexican goods, but by an amount *less than unity*. The greater is the number of Chinese varieties N_y—reflecting more competition from China—the smaller is this pass-through coefficient. From the second equation, the rise in the dollar price of Mexican goods also induces a rise in the dollar price of Chinese goods, even though its exchange rate is fixed. The result is obtained because Chinese firms respond to the rise in Mexican prices by increasing their own prices. The amount by which Chinese prices rise is smaller, however, as the number of Mexican varieties shrinks.

Pass-through of the Multilateral Exchange Rate

So far we have solved for the pass-through of the dollar/peso rate to the dollar prices of Mexican and Chinese goods. In practice, pass-through is often measured using multilateral (aggregate) import prices and exchange rates. To achieve that here, define the import price and multilateral exchange rate by taking trade-weighted shares:

$$\ln P_m \equiv (s_x N_x)\ln(e_x p_x) + (s_y N_y)\ln(\overline{e}_y p_y),$$

$$\ln E_m \equiv (s_x N_x)\ln(e_x) + (s_y N_y)\ln(\overline{e}_y).$$

The weights using in these aggregates are the total share of US imports coming from Mexico ($s_x N_x$) and the total share of imports coming from China ($s_y N_y$). We can treat these shares as constant when differentiating the aggregates (as they will be in any price index). So we obtain the total change in import prices and the multilateral exchange rate:

$$d\ln P_m = (s_x N_x)d\ln(e_x p_x) + (s_y N_y)d\ln(\overline{e}_y p_y),$$

$$d \ln E_m = (s_x N_x) d \ln(e_x),$$

where we make use of the fact that the yuan exchange rate is fixed. Dividing these equations, we obtain the multilateral pass-through of the exchange rate:

$$\frac{d \ln P_m}{d \ln E_m} = 1 - \frac{N_y}{2N-1}\left(\frac{s_x - s_y}{s_x}\right) < 1 \quad \text{iff } (s_x - s_y) > 0.$$

Thus the pass-through of the multilateral exchange rate is less than unity provided that the per-firm (or per-product) share of Mexico exports to the United States exceeds that for China, $(s_x - s_y) > 0$. This condition is guaranteed to hold provided that $A > 0$, so there is a North American bias in favor of Mexico, which we have already assumed. Furthermore we see that the pass-through is reduced when the number of Chinese firms selling into the US market expands. Let us now consider how to estimate the pass-through including this type of interaction effect.

Estimating Equation
Using these various theoretical results, the import price index P_m can be solved as

$$\ln P_m = \frac{1}{\gamma(N-1)} + [1 - B(s_y N_y)] \ln \tilde{E}_m + B(s_y N_y) \ln(\overline{e}_y w_y)$$
$$+ \left(\frac{\alpha_x - \alpha_y}{\gamma}\right) B(s_y N_y)(s_x N_x),$$

where the multilateral exchange rate is

$$\ln \tilde{E}_m \equiv [(s_x N_x) \ln(e_x w_x) + (s_y N_y) \ln(\overline{e}_y w_y)],$$

and the coefficient B is given by

$$B \equiv \frac{(s_x - s_y)}{s_x s_y (2N - 1)} > 0$$

provided that $A > 0$.

We see that the translog expenditure function leads to an approximately log-linear equation for the import price: it is only approximately log-linear because the term B is not a constant but is an endogenous variable that depends on relative wages and numbers of firms.

Notice that the pass-through equation includes an interaction term between the multilateral exchange rate and the Chinese import share. An increase in the *number* of Chinese firms selling in the US market will definitely reduce the pass-through of the exchange rate. Stated differently, an increase in the Chinese *share* will lower the pass-through of the exchange rate provided that the increase in the share reflects an increase in the number of Chinese firms; that is, the increase in share reflects the extensive margin of Chinese exports rather than the intensive margin.[9]

The data we use to estimate this equation is drawn from a set of monthly import prices across 5-digit end-use industries (Feenstra, Reinsdorf, and Slaughter 2008). The same data are used to analyze the Information Technology Agreement, which eliminated tariffs on all high-technology products beginning in 1997, as discussed later. Because the high-tech products require special treatment for tariffs, they are omitted here.

We will gauge Chinese competition by the share of US import purchases coming from China and also Hong Kong. Figure 2.4 shows that average share of Chinese imports grew steadily from 10 percent in 1993 to 22 percent in 2006. We can broaden our analysis to consider the share of imports from not just China but from all countries with a peg to the

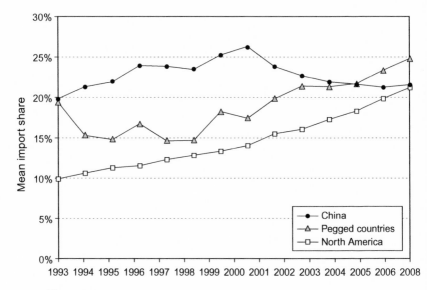

Figure 2.4
Shares of US imports by region of origin. Source: Bergin and Feenstra (2009).

US dollar (Klein and Shambaugh 2006). As seen in figure 2.4, this share initially falls from 20 to about 15 percent, which is explained by the December 1994 peso crisis in Mexico that led to the abandonment of the dollar peg. The peg share subsequently rises to 25 percent by 2006, which follows the growth in the China share.

We first consider a regression of import prices on industry fixed effects, along with a current monthly value and 6 lags of the effective exchange rate, $\text{ExchPPI}_j^{t-\ell}$. The effective exchange rate is the nominal exchange rate times the producer price index from each country, and then averaged over exporting countries. The pass-through regressions should also include prices of goods that compete with the imports, such as domestic US prices. Here we include the US export prices P_{Xj}^t in each 5-digit end-use industry.

The estimate of this regression, reported in the first column of table 2.5, shows incomplete pass-through of exchange rates of 0.21, with a similar coefficient on the export price. The remaining specifications test the effect of Chinese

Table 2.5
Pass-through regressions using the multilateral exchange rate dependent variable: Import price index

	Using China's share			
Exchange rate	0.208**	0.241**	0.341**	0.348**
	(0.009)	(0.009)	(0.012)	(0.012)
Export price	0.224**	0.275**	0.224**	0.157**
	(0.016)	(0.016)	(0.016)	(0.016)
China's share		−0.035**	−0.565**	−0.340**
*Exchange rate		(0.003)	(0.043)	(0.043)
China's share			2.593**	2.056**
			(0.212)	(0.205)
Import tariff				−0.013
				(0.084)
China's share				−0.001**
*Time				(0.000)
China's share				−0.007
*(1 − China's share)				(0.052)
R^2	0.81	0.82	0.83	0.85
N	2,694	2,694	2,694	2,694

Source: Bergin and Feenstra (2009).
Notes: * significant at 5 percent, ** significant at 1 percent; standard errors are in parentheses. Regression specification is run over 23 five-digit end-use categories within consumer goods, capital goods, autos, and chemicals (end-use columns 2–4) for which no imports are covered by the Information Technology Agreement, from September 1993 to December 2006. OLS is estimated with six lags of the exchange rate and fixed effects for five-digit end-use categories.

competition on pass-through, by interacting the exchange rate with the share of Chinese imports in each end-use category:

$$\ln P_{Mj}^t = \alpha_j + \sum_{\ell=0}^{6} \beta_\ell \text{ExchPPI}_j^{t-\ell} + \sum_{\ell=0}^{6} \delta_\ell [\text{ExchPPI}_j^{t-\ell} \times \text{Share}_{j\text{china}}^t]$$
$$+ \gamma \ln P_{Xj}^t + \theta' Z_j^t + \varepsilon_{jt}.$$

The sum of the coefficients δ_ℓ on the interaction term is the incremental pass-through due to changing the China share from zero to one. The additional terms Z_j^t appearing in this regression are control variables such as imports tariffs, the Chinese share of imports, and other terms suggested by the theory.

In the second regression of table 2.5 we include the interaction between the exchange rate and the Chinese import share. The estimate of the interaction term is negative but small in magnitude. The third regression includes the Chinese import share itself as a control. We also include import tariffs; even though the import prices are tariff-free, changes in the tariff levels will still affect import prices under imperfect competition, as in our model. In that case the interaction term of the exchange rate with the Chinese share becomes much larger in magnitude, with a coefficient of −0.57, and this is statistically significant. In the next regressions we consider further adding other controls suggested by the theory, which reduces the magnitude of coefficient on the interaction term somewhat.

We next consider broadening the import share beyond just China to include all countries with pegged exchange rates to the dollar. The results, reported in table 2.6, show pass-through coefficients that are similar to the earlier specification. We conclude that our analysis applies more broadly

Table 2.6
Pass-through regressions using the multilateral exchange rate dependent variable: Import price index

	Using pegged share			
Exchange rate	0.208**	0.227**	0.349**	0.341**
	(0.009)	(0.009)	(0.013)	(0.013)
Export price	0.224**	0.229**	0.187**	0.204**
	(0.016)	(0.016)	(0.015)	(0.015)
Pegged share		−0.015**	−0.510**	−0.264**
*Exchange rate		(0.002)	(0.037)	(0.039)
Pegged share			2.376**	1.363**
			(0.176)	(0.185)
Import tariff				−0.012
				(0.086)
Pegged share				−0.001**
*Time				(0.000)
Pegged share				0.032
*(1 − Pegged share)				(0.041)
R^2	0.81	0.81	0.83	0.84
N	2,694	2,694	2,694	2,694

Source: Bergin and Feenstra (2009).
Note: * significant at 5 percent, ** significant at 1 percent; standard errors are in parentheses. See table 2.5 for further notes.

than just to China, namely to trade with pegged countries more generally.

To summarize, we have shown here that the increased exports from China to the United States, which consist in large part of offshored activities, play a significant role in the pass-through of the dollar exchange rate to US import prices. As the dollar has fallen in recent years, import prices have not risen by as much as expected. Our argument is that the competition from Chinese producers has limited the price increases that could be expected from other, floating rate countries, such as Mexico. Depending on the exact regression, the rising share of trade from China, or from all countries with fixed exchange rates, can explain a decline in pass-through between one-sixth and one-third of its initial size (Bergin and Feenstra 2009). Of course, with import prices rising less than expected, overall US inflation is also moderated, which is a macroeconomic consequence of increased globalization.

Terms of Trade and Productivity

Let us turn now to a third macroeconomic consequence of offshoring, and that is its impact on the terms of trade and productivity. This impact has been the focus of some attention in the popular press in the United States, with an article in *Business Week* by Michael Mandel (2007) entitled "The Real Costs of Offshoring." The costs that its author is referring to are the import competition created by offshoring and the potential impact on unemployment. I would instead see that import competition as a benefit rather than a cost, because it lowers import prices and therefore raises the terms of trade. The link between terms of trade changes and productivity growth is a topic of current research that I will summarize. But before that, let me digress to consider the potential unemployment that might be created by import competition. Does this unemployment create social costs that are missing in our trade models?

Current research on unemployment in trade models depends on either "fair wages" (wages above the market clearing level) or search frictions.[10] Recent theoretical work has put search frictions in models of offshoring. One paper (Mitra and Ranjan 2007) finds that unemployment is actually reduced due to offshoring because the cost-savings for firms leads them to expand employment. More general treatments of trade and unemployment are provided by Elhanan Helpman et al. (2007, 2008a,b), who find that although openness to trade can increase unemployment, the gains from trade remain positive.

With this range of theoretical results, the real test comes from the empirical side. On the one hand, we have the numbers of Alan Blinder (2007), who believes that two or three times the number of jobs in US manufacturing (which are now 14 million) are "offshorable" from the entire economy, meaning that they consist of tasks that are routine enough to be done by a trained worker in another country. That very high estimate of offshorable jobs is best thought of as conjecture. On the other hand, we have the careful empirical work of Liu and Trefler (2008), who utilize the Current Population Survey in the United States to link workers who are switching jobs, or becoming unemployed, to their original industries. They find only a very small effect of services offshoring on either their job switching or unemployment, with an offsetting positive impact of "inshoring" on employment rates and earnings. Likewise a very small impact of offshoring on either job switching or unemployment is found by Peter Egger et al. (2007) for Austria and Jakob Munch (2008) for Denmark. In these country studies the unemployment impact of offshoring is not as bad as might be feared, and we do not consider its impact further.

Modern-day Depressions

Let us now return to the third and final macroeconomic topic, which is the impact of the terms of trade on productivity in the United States or other countries. Motivation for this topic comes from a project on Great Depressions of the Twentieth Century, being run at the University of Minnesota

since 2000 under the direction of Timothy Kehoe and Edward
Prescott (Kehoe and Prescott 2002, 2007). In addition to the
experience of many Western countries during the 1930s, this
project identifies a number of little-known modern-day
depressions: in Argentina, Brazil, Chile, and Mexico for the
1970s through the 1990s, New Zealand and Switzerland for
the same period, and to a lesser extent Finland and Japan
during the 1990s. Depressions are defined by a large negative
deviation from the balanced growth path.

Consider the experience of Switzerland. Stagnant growth
in GDP from 1974 to 2000 qualifies Switzerland as having a
depression (Kehoe and Ruhl 2003, 2005). But at the same time
Switzerland experienced a substantial rise in the terms of
trade, as shown in figure 2.5, from 1980 to the mid-1990s.
Because of that rise in the terms of trade, living standards in
Switzerland did not suffer the same slowdown as real GDP,
as conventionally measured. To capture this rise in the terms
of trade on living standards, it is necessary to define a different concept of real GDP, which we can call real gross

Figure 2.5
Terms of trade for Switzerland. Source: OECD Quarterly National
Accounts.

domestic income. It is obtained by deflating nominal GDP *not* by the GDP price deflator but instead by a deflator that reflects the purchasing power of consumers, such as the consumer price index or the domestic absorption price index. That approach is favored by Ulrich Kohli, chief economist at the Swiss National Bank, as well as by Erwin Diewert (Kohli 2004; Diewert and Morrison 1986). Official practice in Switzerland is now to publish real GDI, which is similar to what is called command-basis GDP in the United States (Reinsdorf 2009). The ratio of real GDI to real GDP is a measure of trading gains for the economy. These calculations show that real GDI rose in the period since 1980 in Switzerland, despite the stagnant growth of real GDP. So, if we instead use real GDI as the yardstick for assessing a depression, then arguably it did not occur in Switzerland at all.[11]

The distinction between real GDI and real GDP helps us understand what happened to living standards over time in Switzerland, and a similar distinction can also be made to cross-country measures of real GDP (Feenstra et al. 2009). But there is still the puzzle as to why real GDP or aggregate productivity, as *conventionally* defined, appears to be correlated with the terms of trade. That correlation has been noted in large panel studies of country growth, where adverse terms of trade shock are often associated with slow growth, as in Easterly, Islam, and Stiglitz (2001). That finding runs contrary to the predictions of neoclassical models, as studied by Kehoe and Ruhl (2008), where changes in the terms of trade should not have a first-order impact on real GDP or productivity, at least not when tariffs are small.

Evidence from the United States

To resolve this puzzle, Feenstra, Reinsdorf and Slaughter (2008) have suggested that there are several reasons to think

that the terms of trade for countries are *mismeasured*, and that
this problem will spillover into mismeasurement of productivity growth. To understand this argument, consider the
data for the United States, in figure 2.6. The thin line is productivity growth for the United States. Prior to 1995, as
Robert Solow famously observed, we could see computers
everywhere except in the productivity statistics. That changed
after 1995, when productivity growth picked up by about
one percent each year. What is not as well known is that the
terms of trade for the United States also began to improve at
about the same time. That is shown by the solid line in this
figure, which divides the monthly export price index from
the Bureau of Labor Statistics (BLS) by the monthly import
price index, excluding petroleum. Finally, the bold line is a
reconstructed version of the US terms of trade from 1993 to

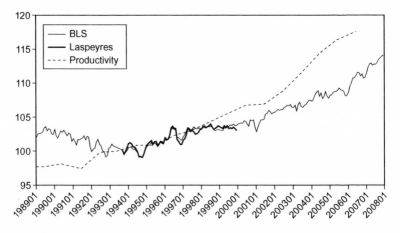

Figure 2.6
US terms of trade and productivity. Source: Feenstra, Reinsdorf, and
Slaughter (2008).

1999, using the disaggregate prices collected from exporting and importing firms, and the same Laspeyres price index formula used by the BLS.

We can see from this diagram that simultaneously with the increase in US productivity growth there was an improvement in the terms of trade, leading to the obvious question as to whether these are connected. Terms of trade changes theoretically should not impact productivity when tariffs are zero. But when tariffs are being reduced, there is a connection between the two. The efficiency gains from a drop in tariffs can be thought of as a movement *around* the production possibilities frontier. Normally we would distinguish such efficiency gains from productivity growth per se, which is an *outward shift* in the production possibilities frontier. But that distinction is not made in practice when measuring aggregate productivity growth because the prices that are used to deflate nominal imports when measuring GDP are *tariff-free* prices. That is, when the BLS measures import prices indexes, and likewise for the statistical agencies in any other country, they ignore tariffs. The reason is that imports within nominal GDP are themselves measured at world prices, and so it is reasoned that the import deflator should be likewise reflect tariff-free prices. But the problem with this conventional accounting practice is that the efficiency gains arising from tariff removal get conflated with productivity gains: in other words, we are not making a clear distinction between the gains from tariff removal, that apply to an open economy, and other sources of productivity gain that apply to a closed economy.

In fact there were some important tariff reductions that occurred in the United States during this period. From 1997 to 1999 tariffs on high-technology goods were eliminated under the Information Technology Agreement (ITA) of the WTO. Because this was a multilateral agreement, and the production of many high-tech goods is fragmented across multiple countries, the tariff reductions can have a *magnified* effect on reducing prices. That theoretical result due to Kei-Mu Yi (2003) is confirmed by Feenstra, Reinsdorf, and Slaughter (2008) when they look at evidence from the ITA. They find that tariff reductions have a *magnified* effect on reducing prices, due to the multilateral nature of the ITA tariff cuts and the fragmentation of production.

The fact that import price deflators used by BLS do not reflect such tariffs cuts can be thought of as one source of mismeasurement in these indexes. There are several other sources of mismeasurement as well. Import price indexes typically use Laspeyres formulas, which have a conventional upward bias, leading to a downward bias in the terms of trade. In addition import price indexes do not reflect the increased *range* of import varieties that are obtained when, for example, there are new supplying countries. As in the Armington assumption, we can presume that countries sell differentiated varieties of a product, so having more trading countries leads to greater import varieties. That increase in the range of varieties would reduce a "true" import price index, even though it is not reflected in conventionally measured import prices indexes.

We can see the impact of these various sources of mismeasurement on the terms of trade in figure 2.7 for the period up to 2000. We repeat the BLS and the reconstructed Laspeyres terms of trade indexes from figure 2.6, and also show several additional series: (1) an exact Törnqvist index for the terms of trade, which used updated trade values as weights, (2) the Törnqvist index that also incorporates tariffs into the import prices, (3) the Törnqvist index that incorporates tariffs

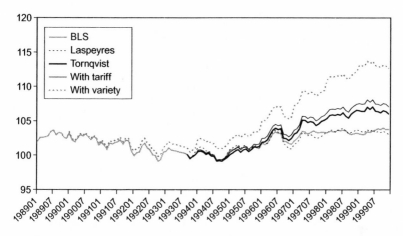

Figure 2.7
Alternative terms of trade indexes. Source: Feenstra, Reinsdorf, and
Slaughter (2008).

and also new sources of import variety, as in Feenstra (1994)
and Broda and Weinstein (2006). The cumulative impact of
these three adjustments to the terms of trade means that the
Törnqvist index, incorporating tariffs and variety, rises at 2.1
percent each year over 1995 to 1999. This is twice as fast as
the BLS terms of trade index, which rises 1.0 percent each
year over 1995 to 2007. Evidently the terms-of-trade gain for
the United States since 1995 has been much higher than suggested by official price indexes.

    With the "true" terms of trade rising faster than official
calculations, it follows that the "true" GDP price deflator will
also rise faster than the official numbers. That is because
rising export prices and falling import prices both increase
the GDP price deflator. By recalculating the GDP price deflator using the adjusted export and import prices, Feenstra,
Reinsdorf, and Slaughter (2008) find that prices rose by

two-tenths of a percent *more* each year after 1995. It follows that real GDP, and therefore productivity growth, rose by two-tenths of a percent *less* each year. The speedup in US productivity growth after 1995 was about one percent each year. So they find that *one-fifth* of that amount actually reflects improved terms of trade, which are incorrectly counted as productivity growth. Consumers have certainly benefited from those terms of trade improvements, but they reflect the gains from trade rather than conventional productivity growth.

Summing up, this evidence from the Information Technology Agreement shows that multilateral tariff cuts had magnified effects on prices in the United States, leading to a fall in import prices that was many times higher than the tariff cut. That is exactly the outcome that we expect in an offshoring model, as shown by Kei-Mu Yi (2003). The industries most affected by the ITA, especially computers, peripherals, semiconductors, and telecommunication equipment, are principally responsible for the differences between the terms of trade indexes that are shown in figure 2.7. Each of these industries have import price indexes that fell faster that the official BLS Laspeyres indexes over 1993 to 1999, once we incorporate the tariff reductions, updated weights as in the Törnqvist indexes, and the import variety adjustment. While the Törnqvist export prices indexes in these industries also fall faster than the official BLS Laspeyres indexes over 1993 to 1999, the bias is greatest on the import side (where the tariff reductions and variety adjustment both pull down import prices further). For these reasons we obtain the overall gain in the terms of trade shown in figure 2.7, which is much higher for the adjusted price indexes that in the official BLS indexes. By incorporating these revised price indexes for imports and exports into the GDP deflator, we find that a portion of the perceived productivity growth in the United States since 1995 is actually due to improvements in the terms of trade. We conclude that the evidence presented for the ITA shows how tariffs reductions under offshoring can lead to magnified reductions in import prices, and therefore terms of trade gains, that are incorrectly attributed to domestic productivity growth.

Notes

1. Bhagwati (2008, p. 11).

2. See also Rogoff (2003, 2006).

3. Another way to generate endogenous markups is by using the linear-quadratic preferences of Melitz and Ottaviano (2008). One benefit of the translog preferences over the linear-quadratic is that they are homothetic, and also lead to log-linear (rather than linear) demand and pricing equations.

4. This material draws on results up to December 1999 from Feenstra, Reinsdorf, and Slaughter (2008), which is now being updated to 2006 by Feenstra et al. (2009).

5. Kawai and Kuroda (2002, p. 23).

6. See the references in Mishkin (2009) and also the recent work of Auer and Fischer (2008).

7. The translog utility function was introduced by Christensen, Jorgenson, and Lau (1975), and the translog expenditure function was proposed by Diewert (1976, p. 122).

8. See Gust et al. (2006), Ihrig et al. (2006), Marazzi et al. (2005), and other references in Bergin and Feenstra (2009).

9. But an increase in the per-firm share s_y from China will increase rather than reduce pass-through, taking into account the endogeneity of the term B. Because we cannot measure the number of Chinese firms or the per-firm share in the data, the interaction term used in the regression simply relies on the overall Chinese import share.

10. For fair wage models, see Kreickemeier and Nelson (2006) and Egger and Kreickemeier (2009a, b). Search frictions build on the early work of Davidson, Martin, and Matusz (1988, 1999). There is also work combining fair wages with offshoring: see Grossman and Helpman (2009).

11. Kehoe and Ruhl (2005) calculate that when adjustment is made for the terms of trade using real GDI, then the case for Switzerland being in a depression over 1974 to 2000 is borderline.

Conclusions and Directions for Further Research

I began these lectures with the question of whether offshoring represents a new paradigm for trade, or whether the Heckscher–Ohlin framework can be extended to incorporate this new type of trade. While this is, in part, just a rhetorical question, it provides a useful organizing principle. Let me conclude by reviewing some of the main insights from this perspective, and then indicate directions for further research.

In lecture 1, I argued that my work with Gordon Hanson (1996, 1997, 1999) can be viewed as an extension of the HO model with a continuum of goods, with the factors treated as skilled and unskilled labor and with capital included. Hanson and I relabeled the goods as activities, as occurring along the value-chain of an industry. The activities being offshored are those consistent with comparative advantage, that is, those relying on less-skilled labor and taking advantage of lower wages for such workers abroad. This model allows us to predict within-industry shifts in demand toward high-skilled labor, just as occurred in the United States and other countries in the 1980s. Because the model relies on trade in intermediate inputs, and its predictions are consistent with the evidence from US manufacturing, we conclude that the 1980s can be characterized as a decade of *materials offshoring*.

But the evidence for the 1990s in the United States, and for Europe over a longer period, is that it was not just the less-skilled activities that are sent abroad; it was also medium- and high-skilled activities. That fact does not sit well with the comparative advantage-based rationale for offshoring, and requires a specification of the extra costs involved with offshoring. That is where the recent work of Grossman and Rossi-Hansberg (2008a, b) is so useful. By allowing for a rich structure of offshoring costs, we can predict that either the low-skilled activities are offshored or the high-skilled activities are sent abroad, depending on the costs of offshoring. The former case fits the 1980s, and we have shown that the predictions of Grossman and Rossi-Hansberg in that case are similar to Feenstra and Hanson, provided that attention is paid to whether we are assuming that offshoring occurs from a small country or a large country. In contrast, the offshoring of high-skilled activities appears to fit the 1990s, when *services offshoring* had started to become more important. Grossman and Rossi-Hansberg (2008a) predict that it is the lower end of high-skilled activities that will be offshored, namely those with more routine activities and less face-to-face communication. This prediction appears to fit the facts for the 1990s, when US workers began facing more job losses, as documented by Crinò (2009).

The motivating force for both materials and services offshoring is factor price differences across countries, but the way that these differences are reflected in the tasks that are sent abroad depends crucially on the extra costs incorporated by Grossman and Rossi-Hansberg (2008a). This is clearly a new aspect of trade, or of the costs of doing trade, which is an important step beyond the Heckscher-Ohlin model. Grossman and Rossi-Hansberg (2008a, p. 1996) conclude their article by calling for empirical evidence on productivity enhancing effect of offshoring, as well as the relative-price and labor supply effects, which has already begun (Crinò 2008; Sethupathy 2008). I would add that evidence on the structure of offshoring costs is an equally important direction for future research.

In lecture 2, I strayed far beyond the questions normally asked of a trade model, let alone the Heckscher–Ohlin model. For each of the macroeconomic issues considered, I ask what the specific contribution of offshoring is to that issue. For business cycle volatility, there is no question that offshoring is important. The ability to shift production rapidly across borders, as firms frequently do, cannot help but to amplify volatility along with it. The evidence presented was for Mexico and the United States, but this issue is equally important in a European context, as suggested by the work of Tesar (2008).

For price determination, I argued that China is too big a player to ignore. That is certainly the view in Japan, and is receiving attention in the United States as well. The model presented is with variable markups (which can also influence business cycle fluctuations; see Bilbiie, Ghironi, and Melitz 2007) but does not explicitly analyze the role of China as a destination for offshoring. That is a simplification in the theory: the fact that China has been a major source for offshoring is one of the reasons why its exports have grown so fast. And as I explain, the growing share of China in US imports has contributed to the fall in the pass-though of the exchange rates, and therefore kept down prices. The final issue explored in lecture 2 was the link between the terms of trade and productivity. That link does not necessarily depend on offshoring but reflects globalization more generally. My discussion focused on the *mismeasurement* of the terms of trade in the United States, in which case aggregate productivity growth incorrectly includes gains due to improvement in the terms of trade. This issue is important in so far as we want to correctly attribute the source of real income gains for the consumer, namely as due to domestic productivity or international trade. But there are other reasons to think that international trade will have a *direct* impact on the productivity of industries. That is a focus of Grossman and Rossi-Hansberg (2008a, b), as noted above, and appears in other trade models such as Melitz (2003). A new line of theoretical literature suggests additional ways that productivity can be impacted by offshoring, which I discuss below, after first reviewing recent empirical evidence.

Evidence since 2000

Most of my discussion in these lectures dealt with the 1980s and 1990s, but what can be said about the new millennium? The impact of trade on wages after 2000 has received scant attention from trade economists, and this shortcoming deserves to be rectified. Even a glance at the data will show that trends after 2000 are difficult to interpret.

The relative wage and employment of nonproduction/production workers in US manufacturing were shown in figures 1.2 and 1.3. Now for the entire period from 1979 to 2006, these two variables are graphed in figure 3.1. Notice the upward trend in both variables during the 1980s, followed by a continuous increase in the relative wage during the 1990s combined with a fall in the relative employment of nonproduction workers, which I argued was consistent with offshoring of the lower skilled among the workers. However, after 2000 the movement in these variables is very erratic: the

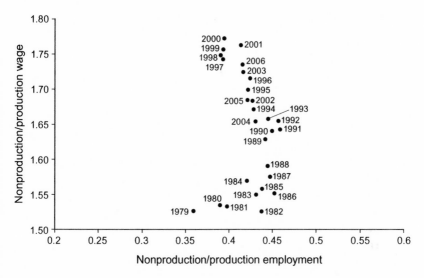

Figure 3.1
Relative wage and employment of nonproduction/production workers in US manufacturing, 1979 to 2006. Source: National Bureau of Economic Research productivity database, updated after 1996 from Bureau of the Census.

relative wage falls over 2000 to 2002, rising in 2003, falling again in 2004, and then rising again in 2005 and 2006. At the same time relative employment adjusts in such a way that the points for 2000 to 2006 fall roughly in the range of those for the 1990s but with greatly increased volatility.

I leave it to future research to explain these erratic movements since 2000. One intriguing observation that should be explored is that most significant changes in the wage and employment patterns for nonproduction/production workers have occurred during *downturns* in the US economy, namely at the beginning of each recent decade. The fall in production employment is especially apparent in figure 3.2

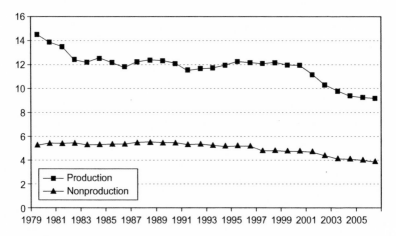

Figure 3.2
Nonproduction and production employment in US manufacturing, 1979 to 2006 (millions of persons). Source: National Bureau of Economic Research productivity database, updated after 1996 from Bureau of the Census.

in the early 1980s and 2000s; in both periods employment fell by about 2.5 million workers. A fall of about one million nonproduction workers has also occurred since 2000. During periods of such structural change it is perhaps not surprising that the relative wage fluctuates as much as it did. Along these lines, Aghion et al. (2005) argue that productivity-enhancing long-term investments are more likely to occur during recessions (in the absence of binding liquidity constraints). It appears that those investments in the United States have also involved a significant re-shuffling of production and nonproduction workers. The suggestion here is that the macroeconomic timing of the employment changes in US manufacturing have not been adequately appreciated by trade economists looking at these shifts, and this feature deserves more attention.

Supermodular Production

Let me turn now from the recent evidence to consider new theory on offshoring. To motivate this, it is useful to start with an unpublished paper by Michael Kremer and Eric Maskin (1996). They begin their paper with the same observation as many others at that time: wage inequality in the United States is increasing. But they propose a new feature of this rising inequality, which is the segregation of workers across firms. They use the example of shifting from General Motors, which uses both skilled and unskilled workers, to an economy based on Microsoft and McDonalds, which segregates skilled and unskilled workers across companies. While the segregation of workers across firms is endogenous, they suggest that it can help us to understand increasing wage inequality.

To develop a model with these features, Kremer and Maskin (1996, p. 4) argue that the production function of a firm should satisfy three conditions, which they describe as:

1. workers of different skills are imperfect substitutes for one another,

2. different tasks within a firm are complementary, and

3. different tasks within a firm are differentially sensitive to skill.

The second of these features—complementarity—is also called supermodularity of the production function.

While Kremer and Maskin's analysis was for a closed economy, it seemed to have a clear application to trade, and to offshoring in particular. I commented on that application in a summary of research that I prepared for the *NBER*

Reporter in 2000. Writing on the topic of "Globalization and Wage," I described their results as follows:[1]

One intriguing channel [for trade to affect wages], described by Michael Kremer and Eric Maskin (1996), involves the hiring of low-skilled and high-skilled workers in a single firm. Under certain assumptions on the technology, this will prop up the wages of the less-skilled workers. But if the overall distribution of workers by skill *widens*, then firms can instead segregate high-skilled and low-skilled workers in different plants, which lowers the latter wages and increases wage *inequality*. While Kremer and Maskin apply their model to a closed economy, the analysis is highly suggestive of foreign outsourcing, whereby firms in one country are able to send abroad the less-skill intensive activities in the production process. Extending the Kremer-Maskin analysis to an open economy is an important research priority.

Perhaps no one read these remarks, but at least I made a good guess on the course of future research! Soon afterward, there have been a number of papers published that address aspects of the problem that Kremer and Maskin proposed. For example, one class of models has managers solving problems for employees (Garicano 2000), which leads to complementarities between these two types of workers, or supermodularity. That type of model has been applied to offshoring, with the managers and employees located in different countries.[2] Another set of papers analyzes trade between economies with supermodular production and more general distributions of worker skills, but without off-shoring.[3] Kremer and Maskin (2006) themselves have a paper that allows for offshoring in a two country model, with only two types of workers in each country. While this illustrates some of the results from their earlier one-country model, the analysis remains special. The latest paper in this line of research, by Arnaud Costinot and Jonathan Vogel (2009), allows for both trade and offshoring, in a more general framework with a continuum of goods and continuum of factors.

The work of Costinot and Vogel (2009) allows the second-moments of the skill distribution to influence trade and therefore factor earnings. It is not just the average amount of factors found in an economy—such as high-skilled and low-skilled individuals, or nonproduction and production workers—but the entire distribution of skills that determines trade. Countries with more diverse endowments of skills can be expected to export goods at the extreme ends of the skill requirements (see also Grossman and Maggi 2000; Grossman 2004). This type of model therefore gives us a rationale for North–North trade, even when average endowments are the same, in addition to North–South trade. And offshoring can be incorporated into a North–North model, too, as in the most recent work of Grossman and Rossi-Hansberg (2008b).

This work incorporating the complementarity between workers of differing skills, or supermodularity of the production function, means that the mix of workers within and across firms has substantial effects on productivity. This is a promising direction for further research, both in theory and estimation. Kremer and Maskin (1996) present an empirical technique to measure the segregation of workers across firms, and its potential impact, which they apply to several countries but not to firms *across* countries. I would expect that offshoring would enable firms to narrow the skill distribution of their workers, by shifting some production overseas. In that case I would further expect that the slope of the wage-effort schedule (as described in the model below) would steepen, as the marginal product of high-effort individuals is increased when their coworkers have similar levels of effort. Indeed Leamer and Thornberg (2000) have shown that the wage-effort schedule in the United States steepened during the 1970s, which they attribute to globalization, meaning a declining price of labor-intensive tradables. I suggest that such an outcome could also be the result of off-shoring combined with supermodular production, which deserves to be explored in future research.

Endogenous Choice of Effort and Product Variety

Besides supermodular production, another way that trade can impact productivity, which has received less attention, is through the endogenous choice of effort by workers themselves. This is the topic of an overlooked paper by Edward Leamer (1999), who embeds the choice of effort into a two-sector Heckscher–Ohlin model. He identifies worker effort as the fundamental source of productivity within firms. While the model he develops is certainly microeconomic in its structure, it can be considered as macroeconomic in its scope, including: "implications for growth, openness, minimum wages, collective bargaining, public support of education, efficiency of state enterprises, the distribution of wealth, childbearing, and much more" (Leamer 1999, p. 1127). I would like to conclude by sketching a model that combines the endogenous choice of effort with supermodularity of the production function, and I will argue that a model of this type can have dramatic implications for the impact of trade on productivity.

Consider an economy with two sectors, and for the moment just a single country. The first sector, denoted by y, consists of a homogeneous good that is mass-produced using an O-ring type of production function (Kremer 1993). For convenience, I will adopt a CES production function defined over the efforts of the various workers:

$$y = L_y \left(\frac{1}{L_y} \sum_{j=1}^{L_y} e_j^\rho \right)^{\alpha/\rho}, \qquad \alpha > \rho > 0,$$

where L_y is the number of workers hired and they each work with effort e_j. This production function is supermodular in the effort levels of the workers, which are complementary:

$$\frac{\partial^2}{\partial e_j \partial e_k} \left(\frac{1}{L_y} \sum_{j=1}^{L_y} e_j^\rho \right)^{\alpha/\rho} > 0 \quad \text{for } \alpha > \rho > 0, j \neq k.$$

Workers are identical, and in equilibrium they will supply the same effort level e_y to this sector. Then the production function is simplified as

$$y = L_y e_y^\alpha,$$

with marginal product

$$w = \frac{\partial y}{\partial L_y} = e_y^\alpha,$$

which is the wage, where we use the mass-produced good as the numéraire.

The other sector, denoted by x, produces differentiated goods with handicraft production. Think of each good as produced by one worker, who must exert a fixed effort level e_0 and then additional effort e_{xi} to obtain the output:

$$x_i = e_{xi} - e_0, \qquad i = 1, \dots, N.$$

The number of workers engaged in handicraft production will equal the number of product varieties, N, so that the full employment condition is

$$L = L_y + N.$$

Utility for the typical worker comes from consuming c_{xi} of each variety $i = 1, \ldots , N$ of the differentiated good, along with c_y of the homogeneous good, with the utility function

$$U = \left(\sum_{i=1}^{N} c_{ix}^{(\sigma-1)/\sigma} \right)^{\beta\sigma/(\sigma-1)} c_y^{1-\beta} - \phi(e)$$

satisfying $\phi' > 0$, $\phi'' > 0$, $\sigma > 1$, and $0 < \beta < 1$. Suppose that a worker has the income of w, and that all the differentiated goods sell of the same price p_x. Then the indirect utility function defined using the price index P is

$$V = \left(\frac{w}{P} \right) - \phi(e), \qquad \text{with } P \equiv B p_x^{\beta} N^{-\beta/(\sigma-1)} ,$$

where $B \equiv \beta^{-\beta} (1-\beta)^{\beta-1}$ is a constant.

Workers can choose to work in handicraft production or in mass-production, and in equilibrium must be indifferent between the two. In mass-production they earn the wage of w, while in handicraft production they earn the sales revenue from their own differentiated product, which is $p_{xi} x_i = p_{xi}(e_{xi} - e_0)$. Then the optimal choice of effort in handicraft production is obtained where the marginal revenue from effort equals the marginal cost:

$$\max_{e_{xi}} \left(\frac{p_{xi}(e_{xi} - e_0)}{P} \right) - \phi(e_{xi}) \Rightarrow \frac{p_x}{P} \left(\frac{\sigma-1}{\sigma} \right) = \phi'(e_x),$$

where we drop the subscript i in the symmetric equilibrium. For the homogeneous good, the wage is $w = e_y^{\alpha}$, so the optimal choice of effort is also obtained where the marginal revenue from effort equals the marginal cost:

$$\max_{e_y} \left(\frac{e_y^{\alpha}}{P} \right) - \phi(e_y) \Rightarrow \left(\frac{\alpha w}{P e_y} \right) = \phi'(e_y).$$

We use these two first-order conditions to solve for the real earnings of workers in each activity:

$$\frac{p_x(e_x - e_0)}{P} = \left(\frac{\sigma}{\sigma - 1}\right)\phi'(e_x)(e_x - e_0) \quad \text{and} \quad \frac{w}{P} = \frac{e_y\phi'(e_y)}{\alpha}.$$

Then the first equilibrium condition is that workers should obtain the same level of utility in each activity:

$$\left(\frac{\sigma}{\sigma - 1}\right)\phi'(e_x)(e_x - e_0) - \phi(e_x) = \frac{e_y\phi'(e_y)}{\alpha} - \phi(e_y).$$

A second equilibrium condition comes from the equality of demand and supply within the differentiated goods sector, using the expenditure share β:

$$\beta(wL_y + Np_xx) = Np_xx.$$

Using the expression for earnings in the two activities, we can simplify this condition as

$$e_y\phi'(e_y) = \left(\frac{N}{L}\right)\left[\frac{\alpha\sigma(\beta - 1)}{(\sigma - 1)\beta}\phi'(e_x)(e_x - e_0) + e_y\phi'(e_y)\right].$$

A final equilibrium condition comes by solving for real earnings within the mass-produced good:

$$\frac{w}{Bp_x^\beta N^{-\beta/(\sigma - 1)}} = \frac{e_y\phi'(e_y)}{\alpha}.$$

Also making use of the price of the differentiated good, $p_{xi}[(\sigma - 1)/\sigma] = P\phi'(e_x)$, and the wages $w = e_y^\alpha$, we obtain

$$e_y^{1-\alpha}\phi'(e_y) = \alpha\left[\frac{(\sigma - 1/\sigma)N^{1/(\sigma - 1)}}{\sigma B^{1/\beta}\phi'(e_x)}\right]^{\beta/(1-\beta)}.$$

These are three equilibrium conditions to solve for the two effort levels and the number of differentiated products. In

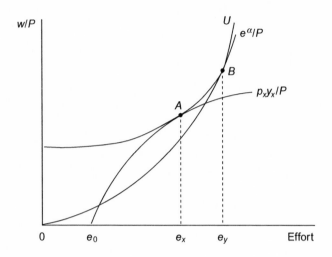

Figure 3.3
High-effort equilibrium

figure 3.3, I show a possible equilibrium for the economy. The indifference curve U is tangent to the curve of real revenue from selling a differentiated product, $p_x y_x / P$, at point A, and to the curve of real wages in the mass-produced good, $w/P = e_y^\alpha / P$, at point B. In the case illustrated notice that the effort in the mass-produced good exceeds that in the handicraft good, $e_0 < e_x < e_y$. I will refer to this outcome as a *high-effort equilibrium*.

There is another possible equilibrium, however, which I show in figure 3.4. In this case there are many fewer varieties of the differentiated product, so the price index is higher and real earnings in either sector are much lower. The indifference curve is now tangent to the curve of real revenue from selling a differentiated product at point C, and is tangent to the curve of real wages at point D. In this case we will have that the effort in the mass-produced good is less than in the

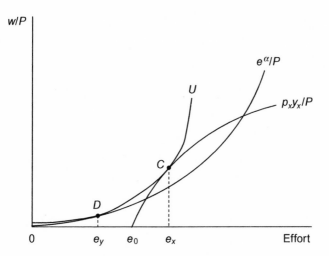

Figure 3.4
Low-effort equilibrium

handicraft good, $e_y < e_0 < e_x$. I will refer to this outcome as a *low-effort equilibrium*.

To distinguish between these two equilibria, we can solve for the borderline case where effort levels in the two activities are equal, $e_x = e_y = e$. In that case the equality of utility in the two activities, together with the equality of effort levels, implies that

$$\left(\frac{\sigma}{\sigma-1}\right)(e-e_0) = \frac{e}{\alpha} \Rightarrow e = \overline{e} \equiv e_0 \frac{(\alpha\sigma)/(\sigma-1)}{(\alpha\sigma)/(\sigma-1)} - 1.$$

This borderline case is well-defined only if α, which is the parameter of the production function, is sufficiently large:

$$\alpha > \left(\frac{\sigma-1}{\sigma}\right)$$

so that $\overline{e}$ exists.

This parameter condition is necessary to observe a low-effort equilibrium, but not sufficient. To determine whether both of these equilibria actually occur, I adopt a specific disutility of effort, which is

$$\phi(e) = \left(\frac{1}{1+\gamma}\right)e^{1+\gamma}, \qquad \gamma \geq 0.$$

An additional restriction on α is needed to ensure that the second-order conditions for the choice of effort levels are satisfied, namely $\alpha < 1+\gamma$.

I have investigated equilibria for a number of parameter values, which can be summarized by the overall parameter Δ:

$$\Delta \equiv [\alpha-(1+\gamma)]\left[\frac{(\sigma-1)(1-\beta)}{\beta}\right] + (1+\gamma)$$

$$(-) \qquad\qquad\qquad (+)$$

If the differentiated goods sector is not too important in consumption, so that β is small or σ is large, then Δ is negative. In that case we have the following result (as proved in the appendix):

Proposition 3.1 If $\Delta < 0$, then there exists a unique equilibrium, with e_x and e_y positive and increasing in L.

The equilibrium in this case can be either a low-effort equilibrium or a high-effort equilibrium, although only one of these holds for given L. With a sufficiently small labor force the economy starts in a low-effort equilibrium, and then it moves smoothly to a high-effort equilibrium as the labor force increases. By making the differentiated goods sector not too important, we have eliminated the possibility of multiple equilibria.

On the other hand, if β is large or σ is small, we obtain the following result:

Proposition 3.2 If $\Delta > 0$, then there can be three equilibria: (1) a zero-effort equilibrium with $e_x = e_y = 0$, (2) a low-effort equilibrium with $e_y < e_0 < e_x$, and (3) a high-effort equilibrium with $e_0 < e_x < e_y$. As $L \to \infty$, effort e_y in the low-effort equilibrium approaches zero, while efforts e_x and e_y in the high-effort equilibrium approach infinity.

I have established this proposition by computing the equilibria for various special cases of the parameters. The low-effort equilibrium certainly gives lower utility to workers than does the high-effort equilibrium, and the zero-effort level gives the lowest utility of all. We might think of the zero-effort equilibrium as the outcome in a preindustrial society, where individuals expend just enough effort to survive (which I have not modeled) but do not contribute toward the market economy.

The fact that this model gives rise to multiple equilibria is suggestive of the findings of Clark (1987), who observes differing levels of effort on the same industrial machines in different locations. One problem with this interpretation, however, is that we expect to find that the low-effort equilibrium is unstable, in the sense that slightly increasing the number of differentiated products would lead to higher returns and more entry into this activity. I have not proved that result formally, but the structure of the model is consistent with an odd number of equilibria, with the "middle" equilibrium being unstable, as we presume is the case. Then this proposition says that a given economy can have both a stable, preindustrial equilibrium, and a stable, high-effort equilibrium. For a large country, however, the zero-effort equilibrium is stable only in a very small neighborhood, because the unstable, low-effort equilibrium is very close to it. So nearly any shock would be enough to move the economy up to the high-effort equilibrium. For large countries we should expect to see them in the high-effort equilibrium, but small countries might be in the zero-effort case.

Let us now bring international trade into the picture. Free trade between countries with identical tastes and technology, in the absence of transport costs, has the same impact as an increase in country size. If there is a unique equilibrium, then opening trade will raise the effort levels in both countries, because of the greater variety of goods available. Utility in both countries will go up because of increased product variety, and because of the induced rise in effort and productivity. The endogenous rise in effort is a source of welfare gain over and above the familiar gains due to increased product varieties.

If there are multiple equilibria, then the story is more complicated. Say that one country is in the high-productivity equilibrium; then it will not be possible for the other country to be in the zero-productivity equilibrium. Rather, the availability of imported goods, as well as the opportunity to market differentiated products abroad, will create an incentive to raise effort levels. So a country that is initially in a preindustrial, zero-effort equilibrium will find that its welfare increases dramatically as it shifts to a high-effort equilibrium. We might think of this shock as an industrial revolution, facilitated by the availability of new differentiated goods. Along these lines Jan de Vries (1994, 2008) has argued persuasively that the industrial revolution was actually an "industrious revolution," made possible by a reorganization of production within the household, shifting from nonmarket to market activities. As workers engaged in factory work, they could use the earnings to purchase an expanding range of products available to middle-income consumers, such as art, books, clocks, and fine furniture. The simple model I have presented is consistent with this story.

Having arrived at this potential "explanation" for the industrial revolution, I have certainly pushed this theory to the limit, and this is a good place to end. I have strayed beyond offshoring to consider the impact of globalization in general, and beyond the second golden age of trade back to the first. Like other modern writers on the industrial revolution, I have emphasized the roles of multiple equilibria, international trade (O'Rourke, Rahman, and Taylor 2007), and product variety in consumption (Greenwood and Uysal 2004). It would be fitting indeed if these new features, combined with supermodular production and endogenous effort, can give us insight into the old but still unanswered questions about the causes of industrialization.

Notes

1. Feenstra (2000–2001).

2. See Antràs, Garicano and Rossi-Hansenberg (2008), and Garicano and Rossi-Hansenberg (2006).

3. See Grossman and Maggi (2000), Grossman (2004), and Manasse and Turrini (2001).

Appendix

Proof of Proposition 1.1

We follow Grossman and Rossi-Hansberg (2008a) in assuming that there are two sectors and two factors, and that the technology in the foreign country is uniformly worse than at home. Let $A^* > 1$ be the Hicks-neutral technological inferiority that applies to both industries in the foreign country. Then, as explained by Grossman and Rossi-Hansberg (2008a), the free trade equilibrium with offshoring satisfies several properties:

1. There is "adjusted factor price equalization," that is, $w\Omega = w^*A^*$ and $q = q^*A^*$.

2. If follows that the relative factor prices $w\Omega/q$ and w^*/q^* are identical in the two countries, so $a_{Lj} = a_{Lj}^*$ and $a_{Hj} = a_{Hj}^*$, $j = 1,2$, where $A^*a_{Lj}^*$ and $A^*a_{Hj}^*$ are the foreign labor requirements per unit of output.

3. Combining $w\Omega = w^*A^*$ with the equilibrium condition $w = \beta t(I)w^*$, we obtain the equilibrium condition $A^* = \beta t(I)\Omega(I) = \beta\left[(1-I)t(I) + \int_0^I t(i)di\right]$, so a fall in β implies a rise in I and a fall in $\Omega(I)$.

4. The world output of the two goods are

$$y_1 + y_1^* = \frac{a_{L2}[H + (H^*/A^*)] - a_{H2}[(L/\Omega) + (L^*/A^*)]}{\Delta_a},$$

$$y_2 + y_2^* = \frac{a_{H1}[(L/\Omega) + (L^*/A^*)] - a_{L1}[H + (H^*/A^*)]}{\Delta_a},$$

where $\Delta_a \equiv a_{H1}a_{L2} - a_{H2}a_{L1} > 0$, with good 1 intensive in high-skilled labor. These expressions are identical to that obtained in a closed economy with endowments $H + (H^*/A^*)$ and $(L/\Omega) + (L^*/A^*)$.

Making use of all these properties, we see that the equilibrium with free trade is identical to a single economy with "effective" wages $\omega = w\Omega = w^*A^*$ and $q = q^*A^*$. Suppose that the two countries have identical Cobb–Douglas utility functions with consumption shares α_1 and α_2 for the two goods. Then the world payments to skilled and unskilled labor are

$$\frac{q[H + (H^*/A^*)]}{G} = \alpha_1\theta_{H1} + \alpha_2\theta_{H2}$$

and

$$\frac{\omega[(L/\Omega) + (L^*/A^*)]}{G} = \alpha_1\theta_{L1} + \alpha_2\theta_{L2},$$

where G denotes world GDP, $\theta_{Lj} \equiv w\Omega a_{Lj}/p_j = w^*A^*a_{Lj}^*/p_j$ is the share of unit-costs going to low-skilled labor, and $\theta_{Hj} \equiv qa_{Hj}/p_j = q^*A^*a_{Hj}^*/p_j$ is the share going to high-skilled labor, for $j = 1, 2$. Dividing these two expressions, we obtain

$$\frac{q[H + (H^*/A^*)]}{\omega[(L/\Omega) + (L^*/A^*)]} = \left(\frac{\alpha_1\theta_{H1} + \alpha_2\theta_{H2}}{\alpha_1\theta_{L1} + \alpha_2\theta_{L2}}\right).$$

Taking natural logs and differentiating, we have

$$(\hat{q} - \hat{\omega}) = -\hat{\Omega}\frac{L/\Omega}{(L/\Omega) + (L^*/A^*)} + \left(\frac{\alpha_1\theta_{H1}}{\alpha_1\theta_{H1} + \alpha_2\theta_{H2}}\right)\hat{\theta}_{H1} + \left(\frac{\alpha_2\theta_{H2}}{\alpha_1\theta_{H1} + \alpha_2\theta_{H2}}\right)\hat{\theta}_{H2}$$
$$- \left(\frac{\alpha_1\theta_{L1}}{\alpha_1\theta_{L1} + \alpha_2\theta_{L2}}\right)\hat{\theta}_{L1} - \left(\frac{\alpha_2\theta_{L2}}{\alpha_1\theta_{L1} + \alpha_2\theta_{L2}}\right)\hat{\theta}_{L2}.$$

The cost shares all depend on the relative wage q/ω, with derivatives $\hat{\theta}_{Hj} = \theta_{Lj}(1 - \sigma_j)(\hat{q} - \hat{\omega})$ and $\hat{\theta}_{Lj} = -\theta_{Hj}(1 - \sigma_j)(\hat{q} - \hat{\omega})$, where σ_j is the elasticity of substitution, $j = 1, 2$. Substituting these above, and grouping terms involving $(\hat{q} - \hat{\omega})$, we obtain

$$(\hat{q} - \hat{\omega})\left\{1 - \left[\frac{(1-\sigma_1)\alpha_1\theta_{H1}\theta_{L1} + (1-\sigma_2)\alpha_2\theta_{H2}\theta_{L2}}{(\alpha_1\theta_{H1} + \alpha_2\theta_{H2})(\alpha_1\theta_{L1} + \alpha_2\theta_{L2})}\right]\right\} = -\hat{\Omega}\frac{L/\Omega}{(L/\Omega) + (L^*/A^*)}.$$

Defining the expression in brackets on the left as B, it satisfies

$$0 \leq B \equiv \left[\frac{(1-\sigma_1)\alpha_1\theta_{H1}\theta_{L1} + (1-\sigma_2)\alpha_2\theta_{H2}\theta_{L2}}{(\alpha_1\theta_{H1} + \alpha_2\theta_{H2})(\alpha_1\theta_{L1} + \alpha_2\theta_{L2})}\right] < 1$$

for $0 \leq \sigma_j \leq 1$, $j = 1, 2$,

where the upper bound of unity is obtained because the denominator can be simplified as

$$(\alpha_1\theta_{H1} + \alpha_2\theta_{H2})(\alpha_1\theta_{L1} + \alpha_2\theta_{L2}) = \alpha_1\theta_{H1}\theta_{L1} + \alpha_2\theta_{H2}\theta_{L2} + \alpha_1\alpha_2(\theta_{H1} - \theta_{H2})^2.$$

Since $\hat{\Omega} < 0$ from property 3 above, then $(\hat{q} - \hat{\omega}) > 0$. However, we are interested in not just the change in the ratio of efficiency wages but change in the actual home wage q/w. To obtain that, we use $\hat{\omega} = \hat{w} + \hat{\Omega}$ and rewrite the expressions above as

$$(\hat{q} - \hat{w})(1 - B) = -\hat{\Omega}\frac{L/\Omega}{(L/\Omega) + (L^*/A^*)} + \hat{\Omega}(1 - B)$$

$$= \hat{\Omega}\left[1 - B - \frac{L/\Omega}{(L/\Omega) + (L^*/A^*)}\right].$$

With $\hat{\Omega} < 0$, it follows that $(\hat{q} - \hat{w}) > 0$ provided that $(1 - B) < (L/\Omega)/(\frac{L}{\Omega} + \frac{L^*}{A^*})$. From the results above, this condition is simplified as

$$\frac{\sigma_1\alpha_1\theta_{H1}\theta_{L1} + \sigma_2\alpha_2\theta_{H2}\theta_{L2}}{(\alpha_1\theta_{H1} + \alpha_2\theta_{H2})(\alpha_1\theta_{L1} + \alpha_2\theta_{L2})} < \frac{L/\Omega}{(L/\Omega) + (L^*/A^*)} -$$

$$\frac{L^*/A^*}{(L/\Omega) + (L^*/A^*)}\left[\frac{\alpha_1\alpha_2(\theta_{H1} - \theta_{H2})^2}{\alpha_1\theta_{H1}\theta_{L1} + \alpha_2\theta_{H2}\theta_{L2}}\right].$$

The condition stated in proposition 1.1 is sufficient to ensure that the inequality above holds. QED

Proof of Proposition 1.2

The first term in the aggregation bias for factor j is

$$\sum_{g=1}^{G} N_g \, \text{cov}_g\,(T_i, a_{ij}) \equiv \sum_{g=1}^{G}\sum_{i\in I_g}\left(T_i - \sum_{i\in I_g}\frac{T_i}{N_g}\right)\left(a_{ij} - \sum_{i\in I_g}\frac{a_{ij}}{N_g}\right)$$

$$= \sum_{g=1}^{G}\sum_{i\in I_g}T_i a_{ij} - \sum_{g=1}^{G}N_g\left(\sum_{i\in I_g}\frac{T_i}{N_g}\right)\left(\sum_{i\in I_g}\frac{a_{ij}}{N_g}\right)$$

$$= \sum_{i=1}^{N}T_i a_{ij} - \sum_{g=1}^{G}\bar{T}_g\left(\sum_{i\in I_g}\frac{a_{ij}}{N_g}\right),$$

where $\bar{T}_g \equiv \sum_{i\in I_g}T_i$. The second term in the aggregation bias for factor j is

$$\sum_{g=1}^{G} \bar{T}_g \sum_{i \in I_g} \left(\frac{1}{N_g} - \lambda_{ig} \right) a_{ij} = \sum_{g=1}^{G} \bar{T}_g \left(\sum_{i \in I_g} \frac{a_{ij}}{N_g} \right) - \sum_{g=1}^{G} \bar{T}_g \left(\sum_{i \in I_g} \lambda_{ig} a_{ij} \right)$$

$$= \sum_{g=1}^{G} \bar{T}_g \left(\sum_{i \in I_g} \frac{a_{ij}}{N_g} \right) - \sum_{g=1}^{G} \bar{T}_g \bar{a}_{gj},$$

where $\bar{a}_{gj} \equiv \left(\sum_{i \in I_g} \lambda_{ig} a_{ij} \right)$ denotes a typical element of $\bar{A}$. Summing these two terms, we obtain $\sum_{i=1}^{N} T_i a_{ij} - \sum_{g=1}^{G} \bar{T}_g \bar{a}_{gj}$, which equals the elements of $AT - \bar{A}\bar{T}$ for factor j. QED

Proof of Proposition 2.1

See Feenstra (2003) and Bergin and Feenstra (2009).

Proof of Proposition 3.1

We make use of the disutility of effort

$$\phi(e) = \left(\frac{1}{1+\gamma} \right) e^{1+\gamma}, \qquad \gamma \geq 0.$$

Substituting this into the equilibrium conditions, we see that the first condition that workers earn the same in each industry becomes

$$\alpha \left(\frac{\sigma}{\sigma-1} \right) e_x^{\gamma} (e_x - e_0) - \left(\frac{\alpha}{1+\gamma} \right) e_x^{1+\gamma} = \left[1 - \left(\frac{\alpha}{1+\gamma} \right) \right] e_y^{1+\gamma}. \tag{A.1}$$

The second equilibrium condition arising from the equality of demand and supply within the differentiated goods sector becomes

$$e_y^{1+\gamma} = \left(\frac{N}{L} \right) \left[\frac{\alpha \sigma (\beta-1)}{(\sigma-1)\beta} e_x^{\gamma} (e_x - e_0) + e_y^{1+\gamma} \right]. \tag{A.2}$$

The final equilibrium condition obtained by solving for real earnings within the mass-produced good becomes

$$e_y^{1-\alpha+\gamma} e_x^{\gamma\beta/(1-\beta)} = \alpha B^{-1/(1-\beta)} \left(\frac{\sigma-1}{\sigma} \right)^{\beta/(1-\beta)} N^{\beta/(1-\beta)(\sigma-1)}, \tag{A.3}$$

which can be rewritten as

$$NA \left(\frac{\sigma-1}{\sigma} \right)^{\sigma-1} = e_y^{(1-\alpha+\gamma)(\sigma-1)(1-\beta)/\beta} e_x^{\gamma(\sigma-1)}, \tag{A.4}$$

where $A \equiv \alpha^{(\sigma-1)(1-\beta)/\beta} B^{-(\sigma-1)/\beta}$.

Substituting (A.4) into (A.2), we obtain

$$e_y^\Delta = \left(\frac{1}{AL}\right)\left(\frac{\sigma}{\sigma-1}\right)^{\sigma-1} e_x^{\gamma(\sigma-1)}\left[\frac{\alpha\sigma(\beta-1)}{(\sigma-1)\beta}e_x^\gamma(e_x-e_0)+e_y^{1+\gamma}\right], \quad (A.5)$$

where $\Delta \equiv [\alpha-(1+\gamma)]\left[\dfrac{(\sigma-1)(1-\beta)}{\beta}\right]+(1+\gamma)$.

From (A.1) we can write $e_y = f(e_x)$, with $f' > 0$ for $f(e_x) \geq 0$ with the properties $e_y = 0$ as

$$e_x = \tilde{e} \equiv e_0\left\{\frac{(1+\gamma)\sigma/(\sigma-1)}{[(1+\gamma)\sigma/(\sigma-1)]-1}\right\}$$

and $e_y \to \infty$ as $e_x \to \infty$. Substituting this function into (A.5), we obtain

$$AL = \left(\frac{\sigma}{\sigma-1}\right)^{\sigma-1} e_x^{\gamma(\sigma-1)}\left[\frac{\alpha\sigma(\beta-1)}{(\sigma-1)\beta}e_x^\gamma(e_x-e_0)+f(e_x)^{1+\gamma}\right]f(e_x)^{-\Delta}. \quad (A.6)$$

For $\Delta < 0$ the right-hand side of this equation is strictly increasing in e_x, and ranges between zero and infinity as e_x ranges between $\tilde{e}$ and infinity. It follows that for any positive value of L, there exists a unique, positive solution for e_x and therefore e_y.

By inspection, it appears that another solution to the three equilibrium conditions is $N = e_x = e_y = 0$. But we can show that solution is not valid for $\Delta < 0$. Specifically, for $\Delta < 0$, we will argue that $N = e_x = e_y = 0$ cannot be a valid solution to the optimal choice of effort in handicraft production, which is obtained when the marginal revenue from effort equals the marginal cost:

$$\max_{e_{xi}}\left(\frac{p_{xi}(e_{xi}-e_0)}{P}\right)-\left(\frac{1}{1+\gamma}\right)e_{xi}^{1+\gamma} \Rightarrow \frac{p_x}{P}\left(\frac{\sigma-1}{\sigma}\right)=e_x^{1+\gamma}. \quad (A.7)$$

To make this argument, we solve for the real revenue (R_x/P) obtained from selling the amount (e_x-e_0) of the differentiated product. Notice that the first-order condition in (A.7) is

$$\frac{R_x}{P(e_x-e_0)}\left(\frac{\sigma-1}{\sigma}\right)=e_x^{1+\gamma}. \quad (A.7')$$

From the various equations of the model, real revenue is obtained as

Table A.1
Parameter choices and equilibria

Parameter	Value
Alpha α	1.0
Beta β	0.5
Gamma γ	1.0
Sigma σ	2.0
Initial effort in x industry e_0	1.0
Calculated delta value Δ	1.0

Equilibria

$L=10$
Equilibrium: $e_x = 0$, $e_y = 0$, $N = 0$
$L = 30$
Equilibrium 1: $e_x = 0$, $e_y = 0$, $N = 0$
Equilibrium 2: $e_x = 1.47$, $e_y = 0.77$, $N = 9.05$
$L = 200$
Equilibrium 1: $e_x = 0$, $e_y = 0$, $N = 0$
Equilibrium 2: $e_x = 1.33$, $e_y = 0.05$, $N = 0.51$
Equilibrium 3: $e_x = 3.25$, $e_y = 4.32$, $N = 112.19$
$L = 1,000$
Equilibrium 1: $e_x = 0$, $e_y = 0$, $N = 0$
Equilibrium 2: $e_x = 1.33$, $e_y = 0.01$, $N = 0.10$
Equilibrium 3: $e_x = 6.86$, $e_y = 10.67$, $N = 585.87$

$$\left(\frac{R_x}{P}\right)^{\sigma} = B^{-(\gamma+1)/(1-\beta)(1-\alpha+\gamma)}\alpha^{[(\gamma+1)/(1-\alpha+\gamma)]-1}\left(\frac{\sigma}{\sigma-1}\right)^{[\beta(\gamma+1)/(1-\beta)(1-\alpha+\gamma)]+\sigma-1}$$
$$\times MN^{[\beta(\gamma+1)/(1-\beta)(1-\alpha+\gamma)(\sigma-1)]-1}e_x^{\gamma(1-\beta)(\sigma-1)-[\gamma\beta(\gamma+1)/(1-\beta)(1-\alpha+\gamma)]}. \tag{A.8}$$

Notice that the exponent on N has the same sign as Δ, by our assumption that $\alpha < 1 + \gamma$. Then for $\Delta < 0$, as $N \to 0$ we see that $(R_x/P) \to \infty$. It follows that as $N \to 0$ and $e_x \to e_0$, the left-hand side of (A.7') approaches infinity, whereas the right-hand side is finite. It follows that we cannot obtain a corner solution where $e_x = e_0$, since an individual obtains higher utility by choosing $e_x > e_0$. By the same argument, choosing $e_x = 0$ is not a valid corner solution to the first-order condition, so the zero-effort equilibrium does not occur. QED

Proof of Proposition 3.2

We provide an example in table A.1 with $\Delta > 0$. Initially for small L the economy has only one equilibrium, with $N = e_x = e_y = 0$. When $L = 30$, there are two equilibria, and when $L = 200$, there are three equilibria: (1) the zero-effort case $N = e_x = e_y = 0$, (2) a low-effort equilibrium with $e_y < e_0 < e_x$, and (3) a high-effort equilibrium with $e_0 < e_x < e_y$. As L grows, effort e_y in the low-effort equilibrium falls and effort levels in the high-effort equilibrium rise, as shown by the $L = 1{,}000$ case.

The finding that effort e_y in the low-effort equilibrium falls in L, while effort levels in the high-effort equilibrium rise in L, are general features of the equilibria when $\Delta > 0$. To show this, we use (A.6) and (A.3) to obtain

$$AL = \left(\frac{\sigma}{\sigma-1}\right)^{\sigma-1} e_x^{\gamma(\sigma-1)} \left\{ \left[\frac{1}{\beta} - \left(\frac{1-\beta}{\beta}\right)\left(\frac{\alpha}{1+\gamma}\right)\right] f(e_x)^{1+\gamma-\Delta} \right.$$
$$\left. + \left(\frac{1-\beta}{\beta}\right)\left(\frac{\alpha}{1+\gamma}\right) e_x^{1+\gamma} f(e_x)^{-\Delta} \right\}. \tag{A.9}$$

As $L \to \infty$, the left-hand side approaches infinity. This implies that $e_y = f(e_x)$ on the right-hand side cannot approach a finite, positive value (since in that case the right-hand side would also approach a finite, positive value). Rather, it must be that $e_y = f(e_x)$ either approaches zero or infinity: both cases are consistent with $L \to \infty$ on the left, since $1 + \gamma - \Delta > 0$. The case $e_y = f(e_x)$ approaches zero is the low-effort equilibrium, and the case $e_y = f(e_x)$ approaches infinity is the high-effort equilibrium. QED

References

Aghion, Philippe, George-Marios Angeletos, Abhijit Banerjee, and Kalina Manova. 2005. Volatility and growth: Credit constraints and the composition of investment. NBER working paper 1349. Cambridge, MA.

Amiti, Mary, and Shang-Jin Wei. 2005a. Service offshoring, productivity, and employment: Evidence from the United States. IMF working paper 05/238. Washington, DC.

Amiti, Mary, and Shang-Jin Wei. 2005b. Fear of service outsourcing: Is it justified? *Econ. Policy* 20 (42): 308–47.

Amiti, Mary, and Shang-Jin Wei. 2006. Service offshoring and productivity: Evidence from the United States. NBER working paper 11926. Cambridge, MA.

Antràs, Pol. 2003. Firms, contracts, and trade structure. *Q. J. Econ.* 118: 1375–1418.

Antràs, Pol. 2005. Incomplete contracts and the product cycle. *Am. Econ. Rev.* 95: 1054–73.

Antràs, Pol, Luis Garicano, and Esteban Rossi-Hansenberg. 2006. Offshoring in a knowledge economy. *Q. J. Econ.* 121: 31–77.

Antràs, Pol, Luis Garicano, and Esteban Rossi-Hansenberg. 2009. Organizing offshoring: Middle managers and communication costs. In E. Helpman, D. Marin, and T. Verdier, eds., *The Organization of Firms in a Global Economy*. Cambridge: Narvard University Press, pp. 311–39.

Antràs, Pol, and Elhanan Helpman. 2004. Global sourcing. *J. Polit. Econ.* 112: 552–80.

Arndt, Sven. 1997. Globalization and the open economy. *N. Am. J. Econ. Finance* 8: 71–79.

Auer, Raphael, and Andreas M. Fischer. 2008. The effect of trade with low-income countries on U.S. Industry. Mimeo. Swiss National Bank, Berne.

Autor, David H., Lawrence F. Katz, and Melissa S. Kearney. 2008. Trends in U.S. wage inequality: Revising the revisionists. *Rev. Econ. Stat.* 90(2): 300–23.

Baldwin, Robert E. 1971. Determinants of the commodity structure of U.S. trade. *Am. Econ. Rev.* 61: 126–46.

Becker, Sascha O., Karolina Ekholm, Marc-Andreas Muendler, and Robert Jaeckle. 2005. Location choice and employment decisions: A comparison of German and Swedish multinationals. *Rev. World Econ.* 141: 693–731.

Bergin, Paul R., and Robert C. Feenstra. 2009. Pass-through of exchange rates and competition between fixers and floaters. *J. Mon. Cred. Bank.* 41 (s1): 35–70.

Bergin, Paul R., Robert C. Feenstra, and Gordon H. Hanson. 2007. Outsourcing and volatility. NBER working paper 13144. Cambridge. MA.

Bergin, Paul R., Robert C. Feenstra, and Gordon H. Hanson. 2009a. (forthcoming). Offshoring and volatility: Evidence from Mexico's *Maquiladora* industry. *Am. Econ. Rev.* 99 (4): 1664–71.

Bergin, Paul R., Robert C. Feenstra, and Gordon H. Hanson. 2009b. Volatility due to offshoring: Theory and evidence. Mimeo. University of California, Davis and San Diego.

Berman, Eli, John Bound, and Zvi Griliches. 1994. Changes in the demand for skilled labor within U.S. manufacturing: Evidence from the Annual Survey of Manufactures. *Q. J. Econ.* 104: 367–98.

Berman, Eli, John Bound, and Stephen Machin. 1998. Implications of skill-biased technological change: International evidence. *Q. J. Econ.* 113: 1245–80.

Bhagwati, Jagdish N. 1997. A new epoch? *New Republic*, May 19, 1997, 36–41. Reprinted in Jagdish Bhagwati. 1998. *A Stream of Windows: Unsettling Reflections on Trade, Immigration and Democracy.* Cambridge: MIT Press, pp. 3–28.

Bhagwati, Jagdish N. 2007. Technology, not globalization, is driving wages down. *Financial Times*, January 4, p. 11.

Bhagwati, Jagdish N. 2008. The selfish hegemon must offer a new deal on trade. *Financial Times*, August 20, p. 11.

Bhagwati, Jagdish N., Arvind Panagariya, and T. N. Srinivasan. 2004. Muddles over outsourcing. *J. Econ. Perspect.* 18: 93–114.

Blinder, Alan S. 2006. Offshoring: The next industrial revolution? *Foreign Aff.* 85: 113–28.

Blomstrom, Magnus, Gunnar Fors, and Robert E. Lipsey. 1997. Foreign direct investment and employment: Home country experience in the United States and Sweden. *Econ. J.* 107: 1787–97.

Bilbiie, Florin, Fabio Ghironi, and Marc Melitz. 2007. Endogenous entry, product variety, and business cycles. Princeton University. Available at: http://www.princeton.edu/~mmelitz/papers/BGMRBC07_0413_figs.pdf

Broda, Christian, and David E. Weinstein. 2006. Globalization and the gains from variety. *Q. J. Econ.* 121: 541–85.

Buch, Claudia M., Jörg Döpke, and Harald Strotmann. 2007. Does export openness increase firm-level volatility? Mimeo. University of Tübingen, Deutsche Bundesbank, and Institute for Applied Economic Research IAW.

Burstein, Ariel, Christopher Kurz, and Linda Tesar. 2008. Trade, production sharing and the international transmission of business cycles. *Journal of Monetary Economics* 44 (4): 775–95.

Card, David, and John E. DiNardo. 2002. Skill-biased technological change and rising wage inequality: Some problems and puzzles. *J. Labor Econ.* 20: 733–83.

Christensen, Laurits R., Dale W. Jorgenson, and Lawrence J. Lau. 1975. Transcendental logarithmic utility functions. *Am. Econ. Rev.* 65: 367–83.

Clark, Gregory. 1987. Why isn't the whole world developed? Lessons from the cotton mills. *J. Econ. Hist.* 47: 141–73.

Costinot, Arnaud, and Jonathan Vogel. 2009. Matching and inequality in the world economy. NBER working paper 14672, January.

Crinò, Rosario. 2007. Skill-biased effects of service offshoring in Western Europe. CESPRI-Bocconi University working paper 205. Milan.

Crinò, Rosario. 2008. Service offshoring and productivity in Western Europe. CESPRI-Bocconi University working paper 220. Milan.

Crinò, Rosario. 2009. Service offshoring and white-collar employment. *Rev. Econ. Stud.*, forthcoming.

Davidson, Carl, Lawrence Martin, and Steven J. Matusz. 1988. The structure of simple general equilibrium models with frictional unemployment. *J. Polit. Econ.* 96: 1267–93.

Davidson, Carl, Lawrence Martin, and Steven J. Matusz. 1999. Trade and search generated unemployment. *J. Int. Econ.* 48: 271–99.

Deardorff, Alan V., and Robert W. Staiger. 1988. An interpretation of the factor content of trade. *J. Int. Econ.* 24: 93–107.

Diewert, W. Erwin. 1976. Exact and superlative index numbers. *J. Econom.* 4: 115–45.

Diewert, W. Erwin, and Catherine J. Morrison. 1986. Adjusting outputs and productivity indexes for changes in the terms of trade. *Econ. J.* 96: 659–79.

Di Giovanni, Julian, and Andrei A. Levchenko. 2009. Trade openness and volatility. *Rev. Econ. Stat.* 91 (3): 558–85.

Di Giovanni, Julian, and Andrei A. Levchenko. 2008. Putting the parts together: Trade, vertical linkages, and business cycle comovement. Discussion paper 580. Ford School of Public Policy, University of Michigan.

Doms, Mark, Timothy Dunne, and Kenneth R. Troske. 1997. Workers, wages, and technology. *Q. J. Econ.* 112: 253–90.

Dornbusch, Rudiger, Stanley Fischer, and Paul Samuelson. 1980. Heckscher-Ohlin trade theory with a continuum of goods. *Q. J. Econ.* 95: 203–24.

Easterly, William R., Roumeen Islam, and Joseph E. Stiglitz. 2001. Shaken and stirred: Explaining growth volatility. In B. Pleskovic and N. Stern, eds., *Annual World Bank Conference on Development Economics 2000*. Washington, DC: World Bank (IBRD), pp. 191–211.

Egger, Harmut, and Udo Kreickemeier. 2008. International fragmentation: Bane or boon for domestic employment? *Eur. Econ. Rev.* 52: 116–32.

Egger, Harmut, and Udo Kreickemeier. 2009a. Fairness, trade, and inequality. GEP research paper 2008/19. University of Nottingham.

Egger, Harmut, and Udo Kreickemeier. 2009b. Firm heterogeneity and the labour market effects of trade liberalisation. *Int. Econ. Rev.* 50 (1): 187–216.

Egger, Peter, Michael Pfaffermayr, and Andrea Weber. 2007. Sectoral adjustment of employment to shifts in outsourcing and trade: Evidence from a dynamic fixed effects multinomial logit model. *J. Appl. Econ.* 22: 559–80.

Feenstra, Robert C. 1994. New product varieties and the measurement of international prices. *Am. Econ. Rev.* 84: 157–77.

Feenstra, Robert C. 2000/2001. Program report of the International Trade and Investment Program. *NBER Reporter*, Winter.

Feenstra, Robert C. 2003. A homothetic utility function for monopolistic competition models, without constant price elasticity. *Econ. Lett.* 78: 79–86.

Feenstra, Robert C., and Gordon H. Hanson. 1996. Foreign investment, outsourcing and relative wages. In R. C. Feenstra, G. M. Grossman, and D. A. Irwin, eds., *The Political Economy of Trade Policy: Papers in Honor of Jagdish Bhagwati*. Cambridge: MIT Press, pp. 89–127.

Feenstra, Robert C., and Gordon H. Hanson. 1997. Foreign direct investment and relative wages: Evidence from Mexico's maquiladoras. *J. Int. Econ.* 42: 371–93.

Feenstra, Robert C., and Gordon H. Hanson. 1999. The impact of outsourcing and high-technology capital on wages: Estimates for the U.S., 1979–1990. *Q. J. Econ.* 114: 907–40.

Feenstra, Robert C., and Gordon H. Hanson. 2000. Aggregation bias in the factor content of trade: Evidence from U.S. manufacturing. *Am. Econ. Rev.* 90 (May): 155–60.

Feenstra, Robert C., Gordon H. Hanson, and Deborah Swenson. 2000. Offshore assembly from the United States: Production characteristics of the 9802 Program. In R. C. Feenstra, ed., *The Impact of International Trade on Wages*. Chicago: University of Chicago Press/NBER, pp. 85–128.

Feenstra, Robert C., Alan Heston, Marcel P. Timmer, and Haiyan Deng. 2009. Estimating real production and expenditures across countries: A proposal for improving the Penn World Tables. *Rev. Econ. Stat.* 91 (1): 201–12.

Feenstra, Robert C., Marshall B. Reinsdorf, and Matthew J. Slaughter. 2008. Effects of terms of trade changes and trade liberalization on the measurement of U.S. productivity growth. Mimeo. University of California, Davis.

Feenstra, Robert C., Benjamin Mandel, Marshall B. Reinsdorf, and Matthew J. Slaughter. 2009. Effects of terms of trade changes and trade liberalization on the measurement of U.S. productivity growth. Mimeo. University of California, Davis.

Garicano, Luis. 2000. Hierarchies and the organization of knowledge in production. *J. Polit. Econ.* 108: 874–904.

Garicano, Luis, and Esteban Ross-Hansberg. 2006. Organization and inequality in a knowledge economy. *Q. J. Econ.* 121: 1383–1435.

Greenwood, Jeremy, and Gokce Uysal. 2004. New goods and the transition to a new economy. NBER working paper 10793. Cambridge, MA.

Grossman, Gene M. 2004. The distribution of talent and the pattern and consequences of international trade. *J. Polit. Econ.* 112: 209–39.

Grossman, Gene M., and Elhanan Helpman. 2009. Fair wages and foreign sourcing. In E. Helpman, D. Marin, and T. Verdier, eds., *Organization of Firms in a Global Economy*. Cambridge: Harvard University Press, pp. 273–310.

Grossman, Gene M., and Giovanni Maggi. 2000. Diversity and trade. *Am. Econ. Rev.* 90: 1255–75.

Grossman, Gene M., and Esteban Rossi-Hansberg. 2006. The rise of offshoring: It's not wine for cloth anymore. In *The New Economic Geography: Effects and Policy Implications*, Jackson Hole, Wyoming, August 24–26. Available at: http://www.kc.frb.org/publicat/sympos/2006/sym06prg.htm.

Grossman, Gene M., and Esteban Rossi-Hansberg. 2008a. A simple theory of offshoring. *Am. Econ. Rev.* 98: 1978–97.

Grossman, Gene M., and Esteban Rossi-Hansberg. 2008b. Task trade between similar countries. NBER working paper 14554. Cambridge, MA.

Grossman, Sanford J., and Oliver D. Hart. 1986. Costs and benefits of ownership: A theory of vertical and lateral integration. *J. Polit. Econ.* 94: 691–719.

Gust, Christopher, Sylvain Leduc, and Robert J. Vigfusson. 2006. Trade integration, competition, and the decline in exchange-rate pass-through. International finance discussion paper 864. Board of Governors of the Federal Reserve System. Washington, DC.

Hart, Oliver D., and John Moore. 1990. Property rights and the nature of the firm. *J. Polit. Econ.* 98: 1119–58.

Helpman, Elhanan. 2006. Trade, FDI, and the organization of firms. *J. Econ. Lit.* 44: 589–630.

Helpman, Elhanan, and Oleg Itskhoki. 2007. Labor market rigidities, trade and unemployment. NBER working paper 13365. Cambridge, MA.

Helpman, Elhanan, Oleg Itskhoki, and Stephen Redding. 2008a. Wages, unemployment and inequality with heterogeneous firms and workers. NBER working paper 14122. Cambridge, MA.

Helpman, Elhanan, Oleg Itskhoki, and Stephen Redding. 2008b. Inequality and unemployment in a global economy. NBER working paper 14478. Cambridge, MA.

Helpman, Elhanan, Dalia Marin, and Thierry Verdier, eds. 2008. *The Organization of Firms in a Global Economy*. Cambridge: Harvard University Press.

Hicks, John. 1932. *The Theory of Wages*. London: Macmillan.

Ihrig, Jane E., Mario Marazzi, and Alexander D. Rothenberg. 2006. Exchange-rate pass-through in the G-7 countries. Board of Governors of the Federal Reserve System International Finance discussion paper 851. Washington, DC.

Jones, Ronald W. 1965. The structure of simple general equilibrium models. *J. Polit. Econ.* 73: 557–72.

Jones, Ronald W. 2000. *Globalization and the Theory of Input Trade*. Cambridge: MIT Press.

Jones, Ronald, and Henryk Kierzkowski. 2001. Globalization and the consequences of international fragmentation. In R. Dornbusch, ed., *Money, Capital Mobility and Trade: Essays in Honor of Robert A. Mundell*. Cambridge: MIT Press.

Katz, Lawrence F., and Kevin M. Murphy. 1992. Changes in relative wages, 1963–1987: Supply and demand factors. *Q. J. Econ.* 107: 35–78.

Kawai, Masahiro, and Haruhiko Kuroda. 2002. Time for a switch to global reflation. *Financial Times*, London, December 2, p. 23.

Kehoe, Timothy J., and Edward C. Prescott. 2002. Great depressions of the 20th century. *Rev. Econ. Dyn.* 5: 1–18.

Kehoe, Timothy J., and Edward C. Prescott. 2007. *Great Depressions of the Twentieth Century*. Minneapolis: Federal Reserve Bank of Minnesota.

Kehoe, Timothy J., and Kim J. Ruhl. 2003. Recent great depressions: Aggregate growth in New Zealand and Switzerland. *New Zealand Econ. Papers* 37: 5–40.

Kehoe, Timothy J., and Kim J. Ruhl. 2005. Is Switzerland in a great depression? *Rev. Econ. Dyn.* 8:759–75.

Kehoe, Timothy J., and Kim J. Ruhl. 2008. Are shocks to the terms of trade shocks to productivity? *Rev. Econ. Dyn.* 11: 804–19.

Klein, Michael W., and Jay Shambaugh. 2006. Fixed exchange rates and trade. *J. Int. Econ.* 70: 359–83.

Kohler, Wilhelm. 2001. A specific-factors view on outsourcing. *N. Am. J. Econ. Finance* 12: 31–53.

Kohler, Wilhelm. 2004. International outsourcing and factor prices with multistage production. *Econ. J.* 114: 166–85.

Kohli, Ulrich. 2004. Real GDP, real domestic income, and terms-of-trade changes." *J. Int. Econ.* 62: 83–106.

Kreickemeier, Udo, and Douglas Nelson. 2006. Fair wages, unemployment and technological change in a global economy. *J. Int. Econ.* 70: 451–69.

Kremer, Michael. 1993. The O-ring theory of economic development. *Q. J. Econ.* 108: 551–75.

Kremer, Michael, and Eric Maskin. 1996. Wage inequality and segregation by skill. NBER working paper 5718. Cambridge, MA.

Kremer, Michael, and Eric Maskin. 2006. Globalization and inequality. Mimeo. Available at: http://www.economics.harvard.edu/faculty/kremer/files/GlobalizationInequality_Oct06.pdf.

Krueger, Alan B. 1997. Labor market shifts and the price puzzle revisited. NBER working paper 5924. Cambridge, MA.

Krugman, Paul. R., 2000. Technology, trade and factor prices. *J. Int. Econ.* 50: 51–71.

Krugman, Paul R. 2008. Trade and wages, reconsidered. *Brookings Panel on Economic Activity* (Spring): 103–37. Available at: http://www.princeton.edu/~pkrugman/pk-bpea-draft.pdf.

Leamer, Edward E. 1994. Trade, wages and revolving door ideas. NBER working paper 4716. Cambridge, MA.

Leamer, Edward E. 1998. In search of Stolper–Samuelson linkages between international trade and lower wages. In S. Collins, ed., *Imports, Exports and the American Worker*. Washington, DC: Brookings Institution, pp. 141–202.

Leamer, Edward E. 1999. Effort, wages and the international division of labor. *J. Polit. Economy* 107 (Pt. 1): 1127–63.

Leamer, Edward E. 2000. What's the use of factor contents? *J. Int. Econ.* 50: 17–50.

Leamer, Edward E., and Christopher F. Thornberg. 2000. A new look at interindustry wage differentials. In R. C. Feenstra, ed., *The Impact of International Trade on Wages*. Chicago: University of Chicago Press / NBER, pp. 37–80.

Lemieux, Thomas. 2006. Increasing residual wage inequality: Composition effects, noisy data or rising demand for skill? *Am. Econ. Rev.* 96: 461–98.

Liu, Runjuan, and Daniel Trefler. 2008. Much ado about nothing: American jobs and the rise of service offshoring to China and India. NBER working paper 14061. Cambridge, MA.

Lorentowicz, Andzelika, Dalia Marin, and Alexander Raubold. 2005. Is human capital losing from outsourcing? Evidence for Austria and Poland. Discussion paper in economics 2005–22. Department of Economics, University of Munich.

Mandel, Michael. 2007. The real cost of offshoring. *Bus. Week*, June 18, pp. 28–34.

Manasse, Paolo, and Alessandro Turrini. 2001. Trade, wages, and "superstars." *J. Int. Econ.* 54: 97–117.

Marin, Dalia. 2004. "A Nation of Poets and Thinkers"—Less so with eastern enlargement? Austria and Germany. Discussion paper in economics 329. Department of Economics, University of Munich.

Marazzi, Mario, Nathan Sheets, Robert J. Vigfusson, Jon Faust, Joseph E. Gagnon, Jaime Marquez, Robert F. Martin, Trevor A. Reeve, and John H. Rogers. 2005. Exchange rate pass-through to U.S. import prices: Some new evidence. International finance discussion paper 833. Board of Governors of the Federal Reserve System, Washington, DC.

Melitz, Marc. 2003. The impact of trade on intra-industry reallocations and aggregate industry productivity. *Econometrica* 71: 1695–1725.

Melitz, Marc J., and Gianmarco I.P. Ottaviano. 2008. Market size, trade, and productivity. *Rev. Econ. Stud.* 75: 295–316.

Mishkin, Frederick. 2009. Globalization, macroeconomic performance, and monetary policy. *J. Mon. Cred. Bank.* 41 (s1): 187–96.

Mitra, Devashish, and Priya Ranjan. 2007. Offshoring and unemployment. NBER working paper 13149. Cambridge, MA.

Munch, Jakob Roland. 2008. Whose job goes abroad? International outsourcing and individual job separations Revised discussion paper 05-11. Department of Economics, University of Copenhagen.

O'Rourke, Kevin H., Ahmed Rahman, and Alan M. Taylor. 2007. Trade, knowledge, and the Industrial Revolution. NBER working paper W13057. Cambridge, MA.

Reinsdorf, Marshall B. 2009. Terms of trade effects: Theory and methods of measurement. Bureau of Economic Analysis working paper 2009-01. Washington, DC.

Rogoff, Kenneth. 2003. Globalization and global disinflation. In *Monetary Policy and Uncertainty: Adapting to a Changing Economy*. Jackson Hole, WY, August 28–30. Kansas City: Federal Reserve Bank of Kansas City. Available at: http://www.kc.frb.org/publicat/sympos/2003/sym03prg.htm.

Rogoff, Kenneth. 2006. Impact of Globalization on Monetary Policy. In *The New Economic Geography: Effects and Policy Implications*, Jackson Hole, WY, August 24–26. Kansas City: Federal Reserve Bank of Kansas City. Available at: http://www.kc.frb.org/publicat/sympos/2006/sym06prg.htm.

Sachs, Jeffrey D., and Howard J. Shatz. 1994. Trade and jobs in U.S. manufacturing. *Brookings Pap. Econ. Act.* 1: 1–84.

Sachs, Jeffrey D., and Howard J. Shatz. 1998. International trade and wage inequality: Some new results. In S. M. Collins, ed., *Imports, Exports, and the American Worker*. Washington, DC: Brookings Institution Press, pp. 215–40.

Schott, Peter K. 2003. One size fits all? Heckscher-Ohlin specialization in global production. *Am. Econ. Rev.* 93: 686–708.

Schott, Peter K. 2004. Across-product versus within-product specialization in international trade. *Q. J. Econ.* 119: 647–78.

Sethupathy, Guru. 2008. Offshoring, wages, and employment: Theory and evidence. Unpublished manuscript. Columbia University.

Sitchinava, Nino. 2008. Trade, technology, and wage inequality: Evidence from U.S. manufacturing, 1989–2004. PhD dissertation. University of Oregon.

Tesar, Linda. 2008. Production sharing and business cycle synchronization in the accession countries. In L. Reichlin and K. West, eds., *NBER International Seminar on Macroeconomics 2006*, vol. 3. Chicago: University of Chicago Press, pp. 195–223.

Trefler, Daniel, and Susan Chun Zhu. 2000. Beyond the algebra of explanation: HOV for the technology age. *Am. Econ. Rev.* 90: 145–49.

Voigtlaender, Nico. 2008. Many sectors meet more skills: Intersectoral linkages and the skill bias of technology. Unpublished manuscript. University of California, Los Angeles.

Yi, Kei-Mu. 2003. Can vertical specialization explain the growth of world trade? *J. Polit. Econ.* 111: 52–102.

Xu, Bin. 2001. Factor bias, sector bias, and the effects of technical progress on relative factor prices. *J. Int. Econ.* 54: 5–26.

Index